Alaska Cruise 1909

Bertha Adele Penny

Compiled by
Constance Taylor

Compilation and layout copyright © 2019 Constance Taylor.

All rights reserved. No part of this book or any subsequent editions may be reproduced, transmitted, broadcast or stored in an informational retrieval system in any form or by any means, graphics, electronic or mechanical, including photocopying or photographing, without the written permission from the publisher, except for the inclusion of brief quotations in an acknowledged review. Requests for permission or further information should be addressed to the publisher.

Library of Congress Control Number 2020900385

ISBN 978-1-888215-79-3

e-book ISBN 978-1-888215-81-6

All photographs and newspaper articles included in this book were found through the Library of Congress online catalog, https://catalog.loc.gov/.

Cover color photograph: Mountains and Reflection, Glacier Bay National Park, Alaska, ©Can Stock Photo / herreid, <a href="https://www.canstockphoto.com">.

Inside cover map: Alaska Steamship Co. The Alaska Line in 1934. [S.l, 1934] Map. <https://www.loc.gov/item/99466709/>.

Printed in the United States
Fathom Publishing Company
PO Box 200448 | Anchorage, Alaska 99520
https://www.fathompublishing.com

Preface

This delightful description of a 1909 cruise to Alaska was written by Bertha Adele Penny. Ms. Penny is the aunt of Mary Taylor, formerly of Napa, California. Mary shared the book with me in 1977. The book remained in a box of my treasures until 2019 when I was sorting old papers and found it again.

I've reset the book for easier reading, added more paragraph breaks and a few commas and updated some spellings. Footnotes explain some terms that are not now frequently used. I've added an index.

Photographs from the early 1900s and newspaper articles about the cruise from the Library of Congress provide additional information about Alaska.

Wendy Kenny was a valuable assistant in preparing this book for publication. I appreciate her contribution.

We hope you enjoy reading about early Alaska tourism.

Constance Taylor
January 2020

List of Illustrations

Standard Pullman car on a deluxe overland limited train. 2
Pullman cars in the early 1900s. 2
San Francisco City Hall in 1909. 4
San Francisco Ferry Building in 1907. 5
San Francisco Cliff House above Seal Rocks in 1907. 6
Mount Shasta and Muir's Peak, California, in 1905. 7
Washington forests with Mt. Rainier in the background. 8
Mt. Rainier in the early 1990s. 9
Leavenworth Echo newspaper described the A.Y.P. Exposition. 10
Hotel Seattle and Totem Pole in Pioneer Square, Seattle, Washington. 12
Seattle, Washington, as viewed from Hotel Washington in 1904. 13
Alaska-Yukon-Pacific Exposition, Seattle, Washington, in 1909. 14
President Taft visits the A. Y. P. Exposition. 15
Olympic Mountain Range, Washington in the early 1900s. 16
Flowers were planted for the A. Y. P. Exposition. 18
The Daily Alaskan announces sailing. 19
Steamship Minnesota and passengers at the Seattle dock in 1907. 20
British Columbia coast and steamer Empress in 1902. 21
Ketchikan, Alaska, waterfront in 1912. 22
Ketchikan, Alaska, Totem Pole in 1913. 24
Front Street, Ketchikan, Alaska, in October 1905. 25
Ketchikan, Alaska, in the late 1800s. 25
Douglas and Gastineau Channel from downtown Juneau, Alaska. 26
Cordova Arrival. 29
Bonanza Copper Mine, Chitina district, Alaska, in the early 1900s. 30

Orca Inlet, near Cordova, Alaska, and railroad trestle and dock.	31
Orca Inlet and Copper River Railroad terminus.	31
Loading copper on the Alameda at Cordova's dock.	32
Viewing the Norris Glacier, Taku Inlet, Alaska, from a steamer.	35
Icebergs from Windsor Glacier, Taku Inlet, Alaska, in 1926.	36
Miles Glacier viewed from the Copper River Railroad in 1916.	37
Tourists viewed the Child's Glacier in the early 1900s.	38
The Aurora Borealis in 1908.	40
Sitka, Alaska, harbor with Three Sisters Mountains.	41
"The Lady of Kazan" in the cathedral in Sitka, Alaska.	42
Juneau, Douglas Island and Gastineau Channel, Alaska.	44
Juneau, Alaska, and the surrounding mountain range.	45
Valdez, Alaska, in the early 1900s.	46
Seward, Alaska, from the bridge in the early 1900s.	46
Valdez at the head of Port Valdez, Alaska, in 1915.	47
Missionary William Duncan at the Metlakatla town library.	49
Metlakatla, British Columbia, School Building in 1915.	50
Tour returns to Seattle.	51
Editors Return from Alaska.	53
The Beaver Herald story covers the Alaska cruise.	54
The Commonwealth editor's review of the Alaska tour.	63
Alaska Information gathered by The Commonwealth.	70

En Route
Observations by the Way

"Now, please don't let me bore you," said the Talkative Lady to the Quiet One, at the very outset of their journey. "I am somewhat inclined to chatter and if I tire you, just say so. You will probably tire me in some other way, so let us make allowance for each other's foibles." So, with such an agreement the Two Travelers started on their eight-thousand-mile journey.

* *

Since the first Pullman car was constructed, there have been strange sights and sounds in sleeping cars. Notwithstanding the fact that every modern device is employed to ensure the comfort of travelers, a sleeper berth is not the little white iron bed at home. Comfort is scarce enough when one has a section all to oneself; but when a conductor attempts to put one man, two women, and a parrot, none of them related even by marriage, in one lower,[1] low, insinuating remarks are apt to be made by someone. In the following instance, happily, the remarks fell on deaf ears for they were made in guttural German.

A little fat Dutchman from the city under the Anheuser Busch[2] was booked for lower eighteen to which the Quiet One had a prior claim. His frau who was short on everything but embonpoint,[3] and who was called Baby by her perspiring lord and master, tried to break into the opposite lower, nine-tenths of which the Talkative Lady owned by already being

---
1 Lower is in reference to the lower berth.
2 City under the Anheuser Busch could be referring to St. Louis, Missouri, where the Anheuser Busch Brewing Company was established, or it could refer to a popular beer garden song of the day, "Under the Anheuser Bush."
3 Plumpness of person: stoutness.

Standard Pullman car on a deluxe overland limited train in the early 1900s.
Detroit Publishing Co. *Standard Pullman car on a deluxe overland limited train.* ca. 1910-1920. Photograph. Lib. of Cong. Washington, *D.C. Lib. of Cong.* Web. Nov. 27, 2019. <https://www.loc.gov/pictures/item/2016800435/>.

Pullman cars in the early 1900s.
Train. ca. 1900-1916. Photograph. Lib. of Cong. Washington, D.C. *Lib. of Cong.* Web. Nov. 27, 2019. <https://www.loc.gov/pictures/item/99614495/>.

comfortably tucked in. There was a slight altercation which was somewhat one-sided, for the Two Travelers maintained a sleepy dignity, while the two angry subjects of Emperor William hissingly spat out something which sounded like a measure from the score of "Götterdämmerung."[1] Persuasion and a hoisting apparatus finally located Baby and her double-decked man in upper seventeen and eighteen, while the parrot, who wanted a cracker much more than she did a berth, was hung in the dressing room.

* *

Morning breaks! The scene is still the Pullman. The three fair young brides and their respective grooms look radiant and smiling. The rest of the dramatis personae look bored and tired. Up stage an anxious looking man is vainly trying to introduce the buttons to the buttonholes in his wife's frock, all the while saying this ?* ! *" ?* ! under his breath.

From the dressing room comes a wail of despair from the Chorus Lady who is en route to the Seattle fair to do the Salome dance[2] on the Pay Streak.[3] She has lost an article of lingerie and demands it with dramatic fervor. It is located, tucked away in her card case. Discovered, center left, Baby, trying to escape from upper seventeen by the ladder route. The scene is beyond description so the curtain rings down to rise on the City which pulled out the tremolo stop three years ago.

My! How Frisco has grown! Scarcely an evidence of the violent chill she suffered in nineteen-six. Immense skyscrapers, business blocks, palatial hotels, well paved streets, magnificent playhouses, artistically beautiful cafes thronged nightly with prosperous looking people. The new Poodle Dog Cafe is so much more attractive than the old place of that name. Its walls are hung with magnificent tapestries and there is the dearest frieze of cupids. The Tate-

---

[1] Götterdämmerung, WWV 86D, is the last in Richard Wagner's cycle of four music dramas titled Der Ring des Nibelungen.

[2] The "Dance of the Seven Veils" is Salome's dance performed before Herod II. It is an elaboration on the biblical story of the execution of John the Baptist, which refers to Salome dancing before the king, but does not give the dance a name.

[3] Pay Streak was the Alaska-Yukon-Pacific Exposition's midway area in 1909.

San Francisco City Hall in 1909.
City Hall, San Francisco, U. S. A. ca. 1909. Stereograph. Lib. of Cong. Washington, D.C. *Lib. of Cong.* Web. Nov. 27, 2019. <https://www.loc.gov/pictures/item/2018646753/>.

Zincan place is paneled and pillared in solid mahogany and the frescoing surely the work of a master hand.

But the most entrancing place of all is the Techau.[1] The interior is Moorish in design, co-mingled with many California suggestions. About the balcony which surrounds the four sides of the cafe proper are rows of orange trees from which hang a profusion of electric light bulbs representing in color and shape ripe oranges. On one side of the lower floor is a pergola with a riot of grape vines trailing over it, the purple fruit hanging in great clusters overhead. The

---

1 Techau Tavern reopened newly remodeled on July 7, 1906. The San Francisco Call reported "the Techau had lived up to its old reputation by the usual excellence of its cuisine and its high class service. ... The tables are of mahogany, the furnishings are of the best, and the silver, the dishes and everything else is of a quality that is in keeping with the reputation of this noted resort."

San Francisco Ferry Building in 1907.
Underwood & Underwood. *The Ferry Building, San Francisco, during street-car men's strike, 1907*. ca. June. 27, 1907. Stereograph. Lib. of Cong. Washington, D.C. *Lib. of Cong.* Web. Nov. 27, 2019. <https://www.loc.gov/pictures/item/2018645399/>.

Hungarian orchestra at the Techau is a great drawing card, for it is led by Rigó,[1] the Hungarian gypsy whom the Princess Chimay[2] gave up home and friends for. It is said the Princess was won by Rigó's soulful playing of the violin. He certainly is master of that instrument and his interpretation of the wild, weird music of his fatherland holds his hearers spellbound.

* *

---

[1] Rigó Jancsi (1858–1927), a famous Hungarian Gypsy (Romani people) violinist who seduced and married Clara Ward, Princess de Caraman-Chimay, the wife of Belgian Prince de Caraman-Chimay.

[2] Clara Ward (1873-1916) was a wealthy American socialite, the only daughter of American millionaire E. B. Ward, who married a prince from Belgium.

San Francisco Cliff House above Seal Rocks in 1907.
H.C. White Co. *The famous Cliff House and Seal Rocks from Sutro Heights, San Francisco, Cal., U. S. A.* 1907. Stereograph. Lib. of Cong. Washington, D.C. *Lib. of Cong.* Web. Nov. 27, 2019. <https://www.loc.gov/pictures/item/2018646206/>.

There was quite a Long Beach gathering on the train to Portland. Coming out of the diner one morning, the Two Travelers ran across dear little Mrs. Adams, she of the smile that won't come off, she who will keep perennially young because she looks out on life through unspoiled eyes; Miss Zech, she of the timid mien, she who loves nature so, in all its various forms; and Miss Knight, wholesome, vivacious, entertaining. Perhaps five tongues did not clatter that day while their owners sat in the parlor car eating great ox-heart Oregon cherries, reading John Muir's Alaskan tree book[1] and exchanging reminiscences. Mrs. Adams was en route to Chicago and New York, Miss Zech to spend a few weeks at northern lakes, while Miss Knight was to spend some time in Portland and later to Chicago.

* *

---

1 **Travels in Alaska** by John Muir.

Already autumn has touched the forests of the northwest with the one kind of blight that enhances and the trees and shrubbery are taking on brilliant tints of crimson and gold. Oregon is superlatively beautiful. The train glides past rock-bedded streams, the water as clear as crystal, the banks tree fringed. The Madrona tree[1] is conspicuous because of its red trunk and green, waxy leaves. There are beautiful valleys, imposing mountains. With serpentine grace the train winds around sudden curves, dashes through tunnels, past small hamlets, hugging close to the mountain side. The breathless

---

1 A tree, notable for its dark redish bark, native to the western coastal areas of North America, from British Columbia to California.

Mount Shasta and Muir's Peak, California, in 1905.
H.C. White Co. *Cloud capped Mount Shasta (14440 ft.) and Muir's Peak, northern California, U.S.A.* ca. 1905. Photograph. Lib. of Cong. Washington, D.C. *Lib. of Cong.* Web. Nov. 27, 2019. <https://www.loc.gov/pictures/item/94505699/>.

Washington forests with Mt. Rainier in the background.
Curtis & Miller, Seattle. *Mt. Rainier from Rickseekers Point with man and woman standing looking over the forest, Mt. Rainier National Park, Washington*. ca. 1911-1920. Photograph. Lib. of Cong. Washington, D.C. *Lib. of Cong.* Web. Nov. 27, 2019. <https://www.loc.gov/pictures/item/90709569/>.

blue of the sky rests gently on the whitened crest of Mt. Shasta, the distant water falls look like threads of silver on a green velvet curtain. Nature, the magician, has let her wand linger lovingly in this wonderful spot.

* *

In Washington there are trees, trees everywhere – alders, birch, spruce – a jungle, a thicket. In many places the undergrowth lines each side of the roadbed, shutting off the view. There are many lumber camps, the huge Moloch[1] of machinery whining and shrieking its way into the heart of huge tree trunks, sounding weirdly above the roar and rumble of the train. There are dusty country roads bordered by "stake and rider" fences, from the interstices of which great nodding clusters of crimson and yellow wild flowers

---

1 Moloch is the biblical name of a Canaanite god associated with child sacrifice, through fire or war.

flaunt their beauty brazenly. There are little towns aggressive in their newness and neatness, the pristine freshness of the cottages unmarred by paint or stain. There are placid pools, their black depths reflecting silhouettes of overhanging tree and fern.

And Mt. Rainier (or Mt. Tacoma as the Tacomans insist on calling it) rearing its hoary head in majestic isolation against the cloudless sky. There are half cleared fields, the blackened stumps of trees mute evidences of the onward march of civilization. There are many grain fields with their neat rows of hay cocks, so peaceful and still that the Talkative Lady insisted she caught a glimpse of Little Boy Blue under one of them fast asleep.

Mt. Rainier in the early 1990s.
Mt. Rainier and Mowich Canyon. ca. 1909-1932. Photograph. Lib. of Cong. Washington, D.C. *Lib. of Cong.* Web. Nov. 27, 2019. <https://www.loc.gov/pictures/item/90709646/>.

10 – Alaska Cruise 1909

THE AUDITORIUM.

The Alaska-Yukon-Pacific Exposition at Seattle, occupying 250 acres of the campus of the University of Washington, will result in benefits for Washington's seat of learning that the University could not have hoped to secure in many years, had not the great fair of 1909 been planned. So the exposition that will exploit Alaska, Hawaii and the Philippines and emphasize the importance of the growing trade with the Orient will leave, after its gates have closed, a large number of permanent structures to constantly remind the people of the Northwest of the Alaska-Yukon-Pacific Exposition and the place it will occupy in the history of the Pacific as the medium through which one-half of the world was brought in such close touch with the other and a tremendous impetus to commercial intercourse given.

Seven buildings on the exposition grounds will be left for use of the University and the auditorium, one of the finest of this group, cost the State of Washington more than $300,000. While the exposition is in progress this building will be used for conventions, congresses and conferences, and its hundreds of seats were in place and the building turned over to the exposition management three months before the opening date of the fair.

Leavenworth Echo newspaper described the A.Y.P. Exposition.
"The Auditorium." *The Leavenworth Echo*, [Leavenworth, Wash.] April 30, 1909. *Lib. of Cong.* Web. Nov. 29, 2019. <https://chroniclingamerica.loc.gov/lccn/sn87093039/1909-04-30/ed-1/seq-6/>.

Seattle
The A.Y.P. Exposition[1]

The very thought of a railroad wreck is fearsome to most people, but, happily, in this day of modern safety devices, the danger is reduced to a minimum and a serious catastrophe rarely occurs. To him who has a keen sense of humor, amusing rather than distressing things happen at such a time. The Two Travelers encountered a spreading rail away up in Washington, with no inconvenience whatever except a five hours' delay. A fellow passenger, however, a woman, was considerably peeved. She had with her as a traveling companion a pet Angora cat which she called Whiskers. She was a married woman and (so she told every passenger who would lend a listening ear) her hubby back East was just as devotedly attached to Whiskers as she was; that it would simply be the death of them if anything happened to the feline; that his catship had liver saute and kidney au naturelle every day served on a real china plate; and so on ad infinitum-ad nauseum.

Well, when the car left the track, the noise and confusion so angered and scared the delicately nurtured Whiskers that he, with his tail swollen considerably beyond normal size and his back describing a semi-circle, spat his way through the wreckage and disappeared into the trackless forest that lined the road bed. The most persistent search failed to locate him. His mistress was hysterical and although there were bruised and shaken human beings all about her, her only thought was for the cat.

Later, when order had succeeded chaos and a station reached where reassuring wires could be sent to anxious ones

---

[1] The Alaska–Yukon–Pacific Exposition was a world's fair held in Seattle in 1909, publicizing the development of the Pacific Northwest.

at home, the cat's owner tearfully dictated the following telegram to her husband, which the conductor sent for her: "Just had a wreck. Am slightly bruised. Don't worry. Whiskers gone." As she signed only her initials, the operator supposed she was a man and said to the conductor: "Say, where the dickens is that guy that lost his whiskers? I'd like to see how he got trimmed."

* *

And so Seattle was reached – that big, husky western city that is growing so fast it is out at the elbows and knees. But, alas! like a spoiled child that has forgotten its manners, so

Hotel Seattle and Totem Pole in Pioneer Square, Seattle, Washington, in 1906.

Kelly, E. W. *Totem pole and Hotel Seattle, Pioneer Square, Seattle Wash.* Mar. 26, 1906. Photograph. Lib. of Cong. Washington, D.C. *Lib. of Cong.* Web. Nov. 27, 2019. < https://www.loc.gov/pictures/item/2019630830/ >.

Seattle, Washington, as viewed from Hotel Washington in 1904.
Keystone View Company. *Seattle, metropolis of the northwest, looking southwest from Hotel Washington, Washington, U.S.A.* May 9, 1904. Photograph. Lib. of Cong. Washington, D.C. *Lib. of Cong.* Web. Nov. 29, 2019. <https://www.loc.gov/pictures/item/2019630813/>.

puffed up over having the A. Y. P. Exposition that it cannot be decent to its neighbors from the south or from any other point, for that matter. The Two Travelers reached there in the gray dawn and went to the hotel where rooms had been reserved for them.

The Talkative Lady was so tired that she fairly threw her Gladstone[1] at the waiting Buttons[2] and demanded to be

---

1 A suitcase with flexible sides on a rigid frame that opens flat into two equal compartments.
2 A bellboy or page in a hotel, a chiefly British expression.

shown her room. The clerk of the demesne,[1] a very superior young thing who was so smug and sleek he looked like a cat who had been stealing cream, managed to send a supercilious glance in her direction and said, curtly, "All full, no rooms for you." "But," insisted the Talkative Lady, a pathetic little droop to her sensitive mouth at being so rudely received, "here is your letter saying rooms would be ready for us." "Madam," thundered the Puny Thing, "you are fifteen minutes late. We would not hold a room five minutes for the president himself." "And I wouldn't stay in your old shack if you had forty rooms!" shouted the Talkative Lady. And so they flounced out outwardly dignified, but wanting awfully to cry on someone's shoulder and each wishing for her own particular specimen of aggressive and combative masculinity down in Southern California who, if he were there, would certainly tweak someone's nose.

* *

And so it was, all over Seattle. Insolence everywhere unless the coin of the realm was proffered for the slightest service. Perhaps their close proximity to our British cousins encourages them to give themselves airs, but the surest

---

[1] In the feudal system, the demesne was all the land which was retained by a lord of the manor for his own use and support, under his own management.

Right
President Taft visits the A. Y. P. Exposition. "President Taft to Visit the A.-Y.-P. Exposition Sept. 29 to Oct. 1." *The Kennewick Courier,* [Kennewick, Wash.] Sept. 24, 1909. *Lib. of Cong.* Web. Nov. 29, 2019. <https://chroniclingamerica.loc.gov/lccn/sn87093029/1909-09-24/ed-1/seq-6>.

Alaska-Yukon-Pacific Exposition, Seattle, Washington, in 1909.
Park, A. J. *1909 Exposition*. 1909. Photograph. Lib. of Cong. Washington, D.C. *Lib. of Cong.* Web. Nov. 27, 2019. <https://www.loc.gov/pictures/item/2007663503/>.

President Taft to Visit the A.-Y.-P. Exposition Sept. 29 to Oct. 1.

THE PRESIDENT WILL ADDRESS A MONSTER CROWD IN THE NATURAL AMPHITHEATRE DURING HIS VISIT TO THE EXPOSITION.

PRESIDENT WILLIAM HOWARD TAFT is to be the principal actor in a varied interesting program, which awaits him upon his arrival at the Alaska-Yukon-Pacific Exposition in Seattle from September 29 to October 1. From the moment Bill Taft sets foot on the paved walks of the exposition he will have to hurry to keep pace with the various events in which he is scheduled to take part. His activities will have a wide range, too. And, then, the president's good nature is proverbial and his lieutenants have sent on word that the president will do his part to make the day a big success. His most formal appearance on the exposition grounds will be at a reception in the Washington state building at the official banquet. Following in line will be his initiation into the Arctic Brotherhood, the Alaska fraternal association. The president will also find time to address a monster crowd in the Natural Amphitheatre, mush down the Pay Streak, attend an elaborate luncheon, visit the United States government buildings and the Igorrote village.

September 30 at the Alaska-Yukon-Pacific Exposition will be one of the president's busiest days in the west and the people will be given every opportunity to see and hear him during his visit to the fair.

deduction is that like the Newly Rich, prosperity has gone to the nearest vacuum – the head – and they are making asses of themselves. But despite its bad manners, Seattle is a great city with infinite resources and its aggressive citizens are building not only for the present but for the future. A few years ago, comparatively speaking, where the city now stands was a little logging town, hemmed in from the outside world with no means of communicating with it except over the broad sea. Now the great iron railway is climbing over the mountains and its many lines reach throughout the union. Only a few years ago isolated from mankind in general, but in this day of generous commercial activity one of the great cities of the Pacific seaboard.

* *

Whom should The Quiet One run across one day in Seattle but Miss Laura Flickinger, at one time stenographer in Shaw & Flint's office. Her many friends in Long Beach will be glad to hear that Miss Flickinger is prospering and is, apparently, in the best of health. She is in Seattle for the summer months, camping on the shore of beautiful Lake Washington with a party of friends. A year or so ago Miss Flickinger took up a desert claim in the Northwest which promises to be very valuable property at no distant day. Her home, until she proves her claim, is in North Yakima, where she is the valued employee of a leading law firm. Miss Flickinger hopes to spend next winter in Long Beach with her sister, Miss Mary Flickinger, of 525 West First street.

Olympic Mountain Range, Washington in the early 1900s.
Romans Photographic Company. *In the heart of the Olympics.* ca. 1907. Photograph. Lib. of Cong. Washington, D.C. *Lib. of Cong.* Web. Nov. 27, 2019. <https://www.loc.gov/pictures/item/2007662939/>.

Another sister, Mrs. Emma White, is a teacher in the Los Angeles schools. The Two Travelers also met, in Seattle, Miss Lutie Major, a former Long Beach girl. Her associates in the First Baptist church and in the various Y. W. C. A. classes will rejoice to know that Miss Major, who has been visiting in the East for a year, is en route to Long Beach where she will reside permanently.

* *

The Alaska-Yukon-Pacific Exposition is not unlike fairs of its ilk except that it is smaller. The same flimsy, temporary structures housing exhibits from various states and countries; the inevitable cascades and fountains; the Pay Streak with its clap trap shows; the noise and cheap excitement; the great throng of people, young and old, feverishly trying to be amused and imagining that visiting the Human Laundry, the House Upside Down, the Tickler, the Joy Wheel, etc., meant having a good time; the going home in the wee small hours with a headache and wondering, next day, what it was that seemed so funny the night before.

* *

The one superlatively beautiful feature of the fair is the landscape gardening, the abundance of beautiful flowers. On the graceful slope of the grounds, masses of flowers bloom, their colors carefully blended into harmonious effect. There are great beds of vari-colored Shirley Poppies[1] waving their brilliant heads on slender tremulous stems; star-eyed pansies, blue, purple, yellow and white, their faces a lot more human than the crowds of wooden individuals who stare past

---
1 A strain of poppies ranging in color from white and pale lilac to pink and red.

PANSIES AND POSIES EVERYWHERE AT A.-Y.-P. EXPOSITION.

In the foreground of the picture is shown the bank which slopes up from Geyser Basin at the Alaska-Yukon-Pacific Exposition, Seattle. Upon it have been planted 300,000 tufted pansy plants, and close up to the bailustrades high-growing plants of bright blossom.

Above Geyser Basin can be seen the banks of the Cascades, and around these are growing 100,000 rose bushes, so selected that there will be a rotation of blooms throughout the Exposition.

Flowers were planted for the A. Y. P. Exposition.
"Pansies and Posies Everywhere at A.-Y.-P. Exposition." *The Ellensburg Dawn*, [Ellensburg, Wash.] July 8, 1909. *Lib. of Cong.* Web. Nov. 29, 2019. <https://chroniclingamerica.loc.gov/lccn/sn88085012/1909-07-08/ed-1/seq-1/>.

them with unseeing eyes, overlooking natural beauty in the search for the artificial; snap dragon, fleur de lis, stock and everywhere in evidence the cactus dahlia, the official flower of the exposition. All through the grounds are tangles of bloom and woodland greens. The exposition has been built in a virgin forest and the buildings rise among firs and cedar and hemlock. The site slopes to two lakes that set like gems in the woods and over all Mt. Rainier looks down from a height of 15,000 feet.

To the west lies the great and glorious range of the Olympics. There are no sunsets in all the world to excel the grandeur of the spectacle on a summer evening when the sun drops down behind the Olympics, bringing out every crag of their rugged rooftree in the dark relief, and painting in a background of crimson and purple and gold behind it.

En Voyage
On Board the Northwestern

The National Editorial Association,[1] a delegated body composed of editorial writers of the United States, held its twenty-fourth annual convention in Seattle, July 1926. Several hundred men and women were in attendance, almost every state in the union being represented. California sent thirteen delegates. The business meetings were held in the administration building on the exposition grounds. Most of the afternoons and all of the evenings were devoted to side trips and sightseeing.

A banquet in the New York building one evening was an enjoyable feature; a trip on the Sound to the Bremerton Navy Yard; a "seeing Seattle" by the automobile route; receptions for the women, smokers for the men; a day at that quaint old British city, Victoria; theatre parties and Pay Streak parties; a day at Tacoma and, by the way, there's quite a friendly rivalry between Seattle and Tacoma. The Tacomans have a slogan which they use everywhere – on sign boards, on letter heads, etc. It is "You'll like Tacoma." The Seattleans point to it and say, "that's a new kind of breakfast food."

* *

EDITORS SAIL FOR CORDOVA

(By United Press.)

SEATTLE, Wash. July 23—The steamer Northwestern will sail for Cordova tomorrow with 125 members of the National Editorial Association on board. The editors have been holding their convention in Seattle.

The Daily Alaskan announces sailing.
"Editors Sail for Cordova" *The Daily Alaskan*, [Skagway, Alaska] July 23, 1909. *Lib. of Cong*. Web. Nov. 29, 2019. <https://chroniclingamerica.loc.gov/lccn/sn82014189/1909-07-23/ed-1/seq-1/>.

---

1 The National Newspaper Association is a Columbia, Missouri based non-profit newspaper trade association founded in 1885 as the National Editorial Association.

20 – Alaska Cruise 1909

A fitting finale to one of the most interesting meetings ever held in the history of the National Editorial Association was the Alaska excursion arranged by W. A. Steele, of Seattle, treasurer of the association. The steamer Northwestern of the Alaska Steamship Company's line, was selected for the trip. It is the best steamship on the Alaska run, capable of accommodating 150 salon passengers, has a crew of 80 men with Capt. A. Croskey, master. The ship sailed July 24 for a twenty days' cruise and carried newspaper representatives from twenty-five states – one hundred and thirty in all – about one-third of the attendance at the Seattle convention.

* *

Steamship Minnesota and passengers at the Seattle dock in 1907.
Underwood & Underwood. *Passengers landing from the Minnesota, largest steamship on Pacific, Seattle, Wash*. Jul. 5, 1907. Photograph. Lib. of Cong. Washington, D.C. *Lib. of Cong.* Web. Nov. 27, 2019.
<https://www.loc.gov/pictures/item/2019630820/>.

(With apologies to Omar[1] and Grace Hortense Tower.)

Some for the glories of the Pines, and some
Sigh for the City's rush and whirl;
Ah, take the Sea and let the mountains go,
Nor heed the clatter of the Summer Girl.
Think, in this ocean Caravansery,[2]
Where doors are open night and day,
How pilgrim after pilgrim, with his Steamer Trunk
Abode his destined hour – then went his way.

As Burton Holmes[3] would say, this Alaskan trip might most appropriately be called an "island itinerary." On this inside cruise the steamship weaves in and out of innumerable small sea-surrounded bits of land rivaling in

---

1 A rewrite of a selection from "The Rubaiyat" of Omar Khayyam.
2 An inn surrounding a court in eastern countries where caravans rest at night.
3 Elias Burton Holmes (1870–1958) was an American traveler, photographer and filmmaker, who coined the term "travelogue."

British Columbia coast and steamer Empress in 1902.
Detroit Publishing Co. *Str. Empress, outward bound.* ca. 1902. Photograph. Lib. of Cong. Washington, D.C. *Lib. of Cong.* Web. Nov. 29, 2019. <https://www.loc.gov/pictures/item/2016802167/>.

beauty the famous Thousand Islands of the St. Lawrence. Following the course of the magnetic needle, the steamer sails through the placid waters of Puget Sound, the great inland sea. For nearly five hundred miles the voyager sails in British waters, along the coast of British Columbia. It is a wonderful water way, as smooth as a great river, on the east the picturesque mainland and on the west the densely forested mountainous islands. From the steamer's deck the view is superb. Charming bays and inlets, hills thickly wooded with coniferous trees to the waterline, mysterious islands pass in panorama. As the boat steams northward the scenery hourly grows more wildly picturesque. Mountain range succeeds mountain range, the snow crowned peaks piercing the clear blue sky.

* *

The Northwestern's first stop in Alaska was at Ketchikan, sub-port of entry, and first port in Alaska, 662 miles north of Seattle. At Ketchikan, commercial Alaska begins – mines, forests and fisheries, churches and societies, courts, newspapers and stores. Beautiful Salmon River runs through the heart of the town and it fairly swarms with salmon trout. The small town of perhaps one thousand inhabitants is built close against the side of a mountain. The steamship folder facetiously says Ketchikan was obliged to climb a hill to obtain a surface area on which to build.

Ketchikan, Alaska, waterfront in 1912.
Winter & Pond. *Ketchikan, Alaska, A.* ca. 1912. Photograph. Lib. of Cong. Washington, D.C. *Lib. of Cong.* Web. Nov. 27, 2019. <https://www.loc.gov/pictures/item/2007661325/>.

Here the first totem poles were seen and one is reminded of Hiawatha[1] –

> *"And they painted on the grave posts*
>
> *Of the graves, yet unforgotten,*
>
> *Each his own ancestral totem,*
>
> *Each the symbol of his household*
>
> *Figures of the bear and reindeer,*
>
> *Of the turtle, crane and beaver."*

Each Indian family has its own particular brand of totem pole, which distinguishes it from other families or clans. They are so hideously ugly they fascinate one. An Indian chief at Ketchikan, whose son recently passed on to the happy hunting grounds, had a totem pole in his door yard and from it hung various articles of clothing formerly belonging to the deceased.

* *

After a week at sea the lure of the mighty deep fills one's veins; the splendid enchantress fascinates and mystifies; the tang of the salt air ascends to the head like wine – it intoxicates, stimulates. The Two Travelers sat aft day after day in a sheltered nook cozily wrapped in rugs and cozily ensconced in comfortable steamer chairs. Bridge whist, which kept some passengers in the saloon, seemed so pitifully inadequate as a diversion when, steaming through

---
1   The Song of Hiawatha, Henry Wadsworth Longfellow.

Ketchikan, Alaska, Totem Pole in 1913.
Curtis & Miller, Seattle. *Totem pole, April 27 1913*. April 27, 1919. Photograph. Lib. of Cong. Washington, D.C. *Lib. of Cong*. Web. Nov. 27, 2019. <https://www.loc.gov/pictures/item/99615187/>.

Front Street, Ketchikan, Alaska, in October 1905.
Front Street; Ketchikan, Alaska. October 5th 1905. January 17, 1906. Photograph. Lib. of Cong. Washington, D.C. *Lib. of Cong.* Web. Nov. 27, 2019. <https://www.loc.gov/pictures/item/2018653779/>.

Ketchikan, Alaska, in the late 1800s.
View of Ketchikan. ca. 1899. Photograph. Lib. of Cong. Washington, D.C. *Lib. of Cong.* Web. Nov. 29, 2019. <https://www.loc.gov/pictures/item/99614611/>.

the thread of wonderful channels close to shore, one could see the line of surf looking like a border of white lace on green velvet; could feast one's eyes on a crystal sea, reflecting, like a silver mirror, the tree-fringed shore and the snow-crowned peaks; to feel the deep silence of the sea – the solitude, the immensity, the grandeur of it all.

(More apologies to Grace Hortense Tower.)

> *And those who husbanded the Ample Meals,*
>
> *And those who flung them to the sea like rain,*
>
> *Alike at last upon the rail do lean;*
>
> *And what is swallowed once must soon come up again.*
>
> *For some we loved – the loveliest and the best,*
>
> *That from these decks, tottering, the steward has ta-en;[1]*
>
> *Have sought their bunks day after day,*
>
> *Have one by one crept greenly to their rest.[2]*

Sea sickness is said to tone up the system wonderfully. The Quiet One is willing to go toniclesss the rest of her natural life rather than suffer another attack of mal-de-mer.[3] She had boasted of being immune – that the sea never

---

1 Old-fashioned, poetic, a contraction of taken.
2 A rewrite of a selection from "The Rubaiyat" of Omar Khayyam.
3 French for seasickness.

Douglas and Gastineau Channel from downtown Juneau, Alaska.
Sheelor, F.W. *Douglas, Alaska, 1914*. 1914. Photograph. Lib. of Cong. Washington, D.C. *Lib. of Cong.* Web. Nov. 27, 2019. < https://www.loc.gov/pictures/item/2007661314/ >.

affected her unpleasantly. There was a dreadfully choppy sea one night and day. The twilight, usually so supremely beautiful, was moody and cold; the night closed in under a sullen, tearful sky, obscuring the moon; the light patter of rain on the decks was soothing to tired nerves but the persistent roll of the boat – each moment becoming more persistent – produced an uncanny and melancholy feeling anything but soothing.

Presently the four winds of heaven seized the boat in a too rough embrace and down, down, down she went and then righted herself in a groggy, wabbly fashion, like a newly born calf learning to walk; buffeted about, this way, then that, timbers creaking and groaning machinery quivering, waves washing over the decks. To quote a young woman from Texas, "It was fierce." Frightened? Never. One cannot be scared and sea sick at the same time. That grinding, gnawing, nauseating, hope-I-may-die feeling is worse than fright. Stateroom sixteen held two women of a greenish cast of countenance all the next day. They claimed they were resting but the only food the stewardess had to furnish them was lemons and dill pickles.

* *

The Purser's table in the dining saloon of the good ship Northwestern was called the "Foolish House" because no matter how the boat rolled and tossed in the trough of the sea there was always a cackle of merriment from that particular quarter. Eleven congenial souls sat around this favored board three times every day – that is, almost every

day. They were Mr. and Mrs. Lyman King of Redlands – he, the editor of the Redlands Review. Mr. and Mrs. King lived in Long Beach a few years ago and have many friends and acquaintances here. Mr. E. P. Clark, editor of the Riverside Press, his wife, Dr. Louise Harvey Clark, noted physician and club woman; Dr. Fred and Dr. Charlotte Baker of San Diego, both physicians and both writers, lecturers and naturalists; Mr. Wirt of Philadelphia, an electrical engineer on his way to Alaska to consummate a huge business deal. The Californians called him Son because he was so young and because his six feet two of muscular length was always ready to fetch and carry for the elderly, unattached ladies of the party.

Miss Potter of Seattle, a dainty girl, reared as carefully as a hot house plant, on her way to the frozen north to become the bride of a civil engineer in Cordova. The knowledge that she was going pioneering was treated as a huge joke by Miss Potter and truly she need have no fear of the coldness and isolation of her future home, for her tender smile, her warm, gentle heart would melt all the icebergs in the Copper River.

The Talkative Lady, the Quiet One, and last and least of all the Purser himself. He was an undersized individual with a head so bald that he looked to be in a perpetual state of décolletage.[1] But what he lacked in height and hair he made up in courtesy and civility. His friends at mess called him Noisy Bill because he was perpetually silent. He broke out into a joke occasionally and one of them follows: "Madam," he said to a California lady whose figure resembles a lead pencil, "you should never remove the plug from the bath tub when you are in the bath." "Why?" asked the astonished, animated clothes prop. "Because you'd surely float out with the water," was the mean response. She retaliated by telling him that she had met his wife in Seattle and that Mrs. Purser showed her a lock of her husband's hair and said she wore it in a locket in memory of him. "Has your husband passed away?" asked the California Lady. "No, but his hair has," replied Mrs. Purser.

---

1 Décolletage is a term used in woman's fashion referring to the upper part of a woman's torso, comprising her neck, shoulders, back and upper chest, that is exposed by the neckline of her clothing.

Coast Tour
The Glaciers, Aurora Borealis, Etc.

"Seward's Folly"[1] away up there in the frozen northwest is producing every year, many times the amount paid for it – seven million of dollars. One gold mine alone, the Treadwell Mine, on Douglas Island, has produced gold valued at five times the purchase price of Alaska. And gold is not the only mineral found in paying quantities. The copper mines are only waiting means of transportation, and that gigantic engineering scheme, the Copper River Railroad, has already pushed its way fifty-three miles into seemingly inaccessible wilderness toward the famous Bonanza Copper Mines in the Chitina district.

The newspaper people paid a visit to Cordova, the terminus of this railway, and were taken for a trip over the shining new rails to the "railway king's" camp. The "king," Michael J. Heney, won fame as the builder of the White Pass and Yukon Railroad, and the Copper River Company lost no time in securing him to direct the building of their road.

> **Editors Arrive in Alaska**
> CORDOVA, Alaska, July 31.—One hundred and fifty members of the National Editorial association arrived here today on the steamer Northwestern and were met by a delegation of business men headed by the mayor. The visitors left immediately on a special train for a trip over the Copper river and Northwestern railroad. A reception and ball was given the visitors tonight upon their return from the trip over the new railroad line.

Cordova Arrival.
"Editors Arrive in Cordova. The Evening Statesman. (Walla Walla, Wash.), Aug. 1, 1909. Chronicling America: Historic American Newspapers. Lib. of Congress. <https://chroniclingamerica.loc.gov/lccn/sn88085421/1909-08-01/ed-1/seq-2/>

Mr. Heney, who is a handsome bachelor – tall, athletic and picturesquely garbed – lives like a prince in his camp. He entertained thirty of the newspaper party at luncheon

---

1 U.S. Secretary of State William H. Seward signed a treaty with Russia to purchase Alaska for $7 million. Despite the bargain price of roughly two cents an acre, the Alaskan purchase in 1867 was ridiculed as "Seward's folly."

Bonanza Copper Mine, Chitina district, Alaska, in the early 1900s.
Bonanza Copper Mine. ca. 1900-1920. Photograph. Lib. of Cong. Washington, D.C. *Lib. of Cong*. Web. Nov. 29, 2019. <https://www.loc.gov/pictures/item/99614369/>.

Orca Inlet, near Cordova, Alaska, and railroad trestle and loading dock.
Railroad trestle with loading dock jutting into bay; snow-capped mountains in background. ca. 1900-1916. Photograph. Lib. of Cong. Washington, D.C. *Lib. of Cong.* Web. Nov. 27, 2019. <https://www.loc.gov/pictures/item/99614509/>.

Orca Inlet and Copper River Railroad terminus.
Ocean terminus of Copper River Railroad. 1916. Photograph. Lib. of Cong. Washington, D.C. *Lib. of Cong.* Web. Nov. 27, 2019. <https://www.loc.gov/pictures/item/99614922/>.

Loading copper on the Alameda at Cordova's dock.
Loading copper on ship. ca. 1900-1916. Photograph. Lib. of Cong. Washington, D.C. *Lib. of Cong.* Web. Nov. 27, 2019. <https://www.loc.gov/pictures/item/99614561/>.

one day and their surprise at the sumptuousness of the spread was not so great when they learned he had a French chef to whom he paid $1200 a year. The camp is complete in all its details and considering the fact that no women are employed or live there, the order and neatness prevailing was a subject for comment. There are, first of all, Mr. Heney's private tent and those of his private secretary, and the camp physician – the last named is paid $10 a day and all expenses – the tents of all the workmen, the kitchen tents and the various dining tents, a finely equipped hospital tent over which the Red Cross flag waves – all of these canvas homes spotlessly white and orderly. Mr. Heney's living tent is sybaritical[1] in its appointments. It is as large as a California bungalow and the floor is covered with skins of Alaskan bears – the snowy white of the Polar bear, the rich brown of the Cinnamon, the curious grayish blue of the Glacier bear, the rich glossy fur of the Black, and on the walls more trophies of the hunt – smaller skins of the Hudson Bay Sable and the tiny black tipped Ermine. Luxurious, deeply-cushioned seats and lounging places filled the spacious room, rare paintings and books everywhere, and on the buffet rare china, cut glass and silver. It was a bit of the luxury of civilization transplanted to a wilderness.

But to go back to the resources of Alaska. Our northwestern possession contains more coal than Pennsylvania; the Katalla oil fields produce oil of the best quality; in one part of Alaska marble is quarried equal to any in the United States and in another district gypsum is mined; asbestos, mica, cinnabar, graphite and bismuth are found; garnets and rubies have been found in the territory and there is a mountain of jade on the Kobuk River.

There are more fish in Alaskan waters than in all the fisheries of the Atlantic coast. If the cans of salmon put up in Alaska were laid end to end, they would reach five times round the earth. The livestock industry of Alaska is confined to reindeer. There are 20,000 there now and the increase is at the rate of $33\frac{1}{3}$ percent per year.

---

[1] Voluptuous, luxurious, wanton.

When the reader learns that reindeer steak is the most delicious meat imaginable and that the reindeer moss upon which the animal feeds grows wild, without cultivation, and that shelter or stabling is unnecessary, he will realize what a gigantic, colossal thing livestock industry in Alaska really is.

Then there are extensive areas of timber which some day will be converted into lumber, for Alaska has vast forests. In these forests are thousands of acres of fruit laden bushes – great pink salmon berries, luscious, abnormally large blueberries, cranberries, currants and strawberries. The bears feast in berry patches and grow fat. The Eskimos preserve the fruit by soaking it in seal oil. Just fancy the mess! In a word, nature has placed the material in Alaska and it remains for man to develop it.

"There is a divinity that shapes our ends, rough hew them as we will," sounds pretty, but is it true? The whole panorama of the world teaches us that Divinity is not engaged in shaping ends. When the All Wise Father finished the Creation, he did all that was necessary for Him to do and left plenty of work for His children, so that they should not be drones. He put valuable minerals deep in the bosom of the earth but he left the digging and the utilizing to us. God said, "Behold, I have given you every herb bearing seed which is upon the face of the earth, and every tree, on which is the fruit of a tree yielding seed," and yet He does not plow or sow or reap or gather the harvest. Man must take up the work left him to do by the Creator – must develop the resources given so abundantly to him.

* *

Probably nothing thrills the visitor to Alaska so much as his first view of the glaciers. The reader of course knows what a glacier is – that it is an immense field or stream of ice formed in a region of perpetual snow and moving slowly down a mountain slope or valley. The upper part of the glacier is compacted snow which lies on the crevassed and serrated mass of solid ice beneath, forming the glacier proper. This snow and ice has been accumulating thousands of years and no one can estimate its depth. The fall of snow in some of the Alaskan coast towns which the newspaper

Viewing the Norris Glacier, Taku Inlet, Alaska, from a steamer.
Keystone View Company. *View of Norris Glacier from steamer, Taku Inlet, Alaska.* ca. 1926. Photograph. Lib. of Cong. Washington, D.C. *Lib. of Cong.* Web. Nov. 27, 2019. <https://www.loc.gov/pictures/item/2017653116/>.

people visited often exceeds sixty-seven feet and the fall in the mountains being relatively larger, is quite beyond comprehension. The snow slides and tumbles down the mountain sides into the ravines and fills the valleys. The constantly increasing weight of this frozen body forces it to move and great icebergs are discharged constantly.

Sailing into Stevens Passage, the steamer encounters icebergs, large and small, reflecting in the brilliant sunlight the most beautiful shades of blue and green. Feeling its way carefully, with engines scarcely moving, the Northwestern approached Taku Glacier. Words seem empty – meaningless – when one attempts to describe this formidable wall of ice. It

Icebergs from Windsor Glacier, Taku Inlet, Alaska, in 1926.
Underwood & Underwood. *The head of Windsor Glacier, Taku Inlet, Alaska*. Feb. 5, 1926. Photograph. Lib. of Cong. Washington, D.C. *Lib. of Cong*. Web. Nov. 27, 2019. <https://www.loc.gov/pictures/item/2017653118/>.

must be seen to be appreciated. It is surely a startling surprise to one sated with routine scenery when he is suddenly brought face to face with this most tremendous force of nature. He is given a new perspective of life and begins to realize how small is human endeavor when compared to the work of nature.

The bold, vertical frontage of Taku Glacier is 200 feet high and one mile wide. The ice of a beautiful intense blue that no other glacier possesses. The front reaches into fifty fathoms of water, and is continually sloughing off icebergs with thunder-like roar. No matter how great the ruin, with acres of ice falling every day, an inexhaustible supply is continually edging forward to take the place of that which falls.

Miles Glacier viewed from the Copper River Railroad in 1916.
Hegg, Eric A. *Miles Glacier*. 1916. Photograph. Lib. of Cong. Washington, D.C. *Lib. of Cong.* Web. Nov. 27, 2019. <https://www.loc.gov/pictures/item/99614942/>.

    The Miles and Childs Glaciers are only four miles apart. These are live glaciers, discharging acres of ice every day. The Childs is a towering, 250-foot wall of solid ice, three miles across the face and is forty miles long. Rex Beach says of it, "I hope never to lose the memory of that first impression." There was Childs Glacier at last, with the ravenous river gnawing at it, a towering wall of solid ice, serrated and seamed – the dead grayness of infinite age upon its face. And so close! We fairly felt its presence before we sensed the chill breath which swept down from it. There were no intervening miles to rob it of its grandeur – its very proximity was terrifying – it was so strange, so unknown, so lifeless, yet so menacing.

* *

    The discipline on shipboard is rigid indeed. At exactly the same hour every morning the decks are washed down. At exactly the same moment three times each day the gong rings for breakfast, luncheon or dinner. On exactly the same day each week the signal is given for fire drill and the

Tourists viewed the Child's Glacier in the early 1900s.
Child's Glacier. ca. 1900-1916. Photograph. Lib. of Cong. Washington, D.C. *Lib. of Cong.* Web. Nov. 27, 2019. <https://www.loc.gov/pictures/item/99614457//>.

sailors swiftly and automatically spring to their tasks. One is reminded of well-oiled and regulated machinery.

To illustrate how they stick to rules a story was told which has been going the rounds of the press and probably is told to the passengers on every trip of every steamship. Off a port one night the night watchman leaned over the ship side in answer to a hail: "Ahoy," he said. "Ahoy," was the reply. "Lower down your ship's ladder, shipmate." "You can't come aboard here tonight," said the watchman. "Lower sway, you lubber," said the voice below, impatiently. "I must come aboard. I'm the Narrows pilot." "I don't care," said the watchman, "if you're Punchus Pilot, I'll stick to the ship's rules."

* *

The most popular man in the official roster of the Northwestern was the chief engineer. He has been, for many years, a sea-faring man and instead of being taciturn, as many are who follow the sea, or coldly aloof, as are the snow-crowned summits that meet his daily vision, he was cordiality itself. Big and brawny, with clear blue eyes, hair slightly silvered at the temples and a few lines – the love-marks of time – on his resolute face, he was the embodiment of courage and force. Although he ruled the many men under his control with a rod of iron and suffered no soldiering, they all adored him. The one startling thing about the chief was his superb profane vocabulary. It was unique and in a class by itself. He called it steamboat talk.

With a fund of general information and absolutely illimitable in his knowledge of Alaskan history and lore, and being good naturedly willing to impart information, he was sought early and late to answer diverse and sundry questions. He told with great glee of a gushing young woman passenger, who when he pointed out to her Mt. St. Elias, that stern sentinel of both American and British possessions – that titanic and majestic mountain that rears its snow-crowned head far above the clouds, she ejaculated, "Ain't it cute." The same young woman, when the steamer was passing the beautiful group of San Juan islands, asked if there was water on the other side of the islands.

* *

At 2 o'clock one morning, the Chief rapped on the window of Number 16 and called out, "Ladies, get up and see the Northern Lights. Hurry, the illumination will not last long." The Talkative Lady opened her eyes long enough to say, "Please go 'way and let me sleep," and sank back, comfy and cozy, in her little bunk, a devotee to the god of dreams. The Quiet One, avid of sleep, yet greedier for this rare view of nature's wonder work, hastily donned kimona and slippers, and scurrying through the saloon, joined the nocturnal watchers on deck. It was a still, cloudless night, the stars hung low down, glittering like jewels on a velvet background. The solemn silence of the night – the limitless solitude – the brooding quiet of the sky seeming to hold itself aloof from things earthly, gave an impression of mystery – unreality. As some writer has said, "It was like curtains drawn over the infinite – like veils let down to conceal mysteries from the imagination of men." A pale pink glow gradually deepening to crimson illumined the north, seemingly emerging from the black waste of waters. The brilliant mass of color lengthened out into rays, the rosy fingers stretching across the sky formed a luminous arch that

The Aurora Borealis in 1908.
The aurora borealis as seen at Dawson, the capitol of Yukon Territory. ca. 1908. Photograph. Lib. of Cong. Washington, D.C. *Lib. of Cong.* Web. Nov. 27, 2019. <https://www.loc.gov/pictures/item/2002706805/>.

spanned the heavens. The black canopy of night hung so low that the breathless watchers on deck felt that they could almost touch it. The North Star, quite dimming the lesser luminaries, shone with glorious refulgence. Suddenly against the horizon a blood red crescent appeared. It was the waning moon and its crimson glow sent a luminous trail across the trackless sea. The scene beggared description. But with the moon's advent, the Aurora Borealis, in which all "the glittering mirrors of the sea were reflecting on trembling rays of rose" sank faintly into pale tints – into soft pastel shades – the grays and pinks growing darker until the black dome overhead and the black sea beneath were unrelieved except by the slender crescent which seemed momentarily to glow more faintly and soon the wan, pale light of an arctic dawn began to chase the shadows away.

Alaska
Coast Towns and Some of its Resources

Southeastern Alaska, the panhandle portion of the great northern territory, is the pioneer section as regards industrial endeavor, since settlements there were flourishing years before the famous gold strikes at Nome. Sitka, the Beautiful, the old capitol of Alaska, was established by Alexander Baranoff[1] in 1804. It is said to be the most picturesquely located of any Alaskan city. It is a quaint old town with a foreign charm that is indescribable. Encircling it are ninety

---

1 Alexander Baranoff (1747-1819) was a Russian trader and merchant, who worked for some time in Siberia. He was recruited by the Shelikov Company for trading in Russian America.

Sitka, Alaska, harbor with Three Sisters Mountains.
Hegg, Eric A. *Three Sisters Mts. (background)*. ca. 1900-1930. Photograph. Lib. of Cong. Washington, D.C. *Lib. of Cong.* Web. Nov. 27, 2019. <https://www.loc.gov/pictures/item/99614781/>.

"The Lady of Kazan" in the cathedral in Sitka, Alaska.
Hegg, Eric A. *Painting of madonna and child called "The Lady of Kazan" in Russian cathedral*. ca. 1900-1930. Photograph. Lib. of Cong. Washington, D.C. *Lib. of Cong.* Web. Nov. 27, 2019. <https://www.loc.gov/pictures/item/99614806/>.

small, green islands, and in the distance, Mt. Edgecombe, an extinct volcano, lifts its snowy crater above the clouds. Sitka was a fur trading post when it belonged to Russia and many priceless furs – otter, ermine, beaver and marten – were shipped across the seas. There is a sense of antiquity about Sitka, an historic setting that distinguishes it from the newer, cruder towns. In the old Greek church, which was built more than a century ago, there are robes and paintings valued at $300,000. Two paintings, "The Madonna" and "The Lord's Supper" were given to the church by a Russian nobleman. It is said that Helen Gould offered a fabulous sum for them at one time. In all the leading towns of Alaska, there are Christian churches. Roman Catholics, Episcopalians, Methodists, Congregationals, Presbyterians and Christian Science all have regular church organizations.

* *

The steamship Northwestern is equipped with a wireless outfit and a Paper was issued each morning containing news from all over the World, as well as local boat news. This paper sold for ten cents a copy and found eager purchasers.

Various forms of amusement were furnished the passengers. There were lectures on various topics, evenings of music, progressive card parties, amateur theatricals and each Sabbath religious services were held, the two ministers on board alternating in conducting the service. During the twenty-one days of life on ship board there was never a dull hour. Long as the days were, lasting from three a.m until ten-thirty p.m., there was always something to interest and amuse.

After the seven o'clock dinner it seemed so strange to have more than three hours of daylight. At that time there was always a group in the bow of the boat happily gazing at the ever-changing panorama, watching the sapphire water roll in symmetrical waves from either side of the Northwestern's graceful bow and waiting, waiting, for the strangeness and vagueness of an Alaskan twilight. The great red disk at the horizon's edge shining so far beyond office hours seemed uncanny – unreal. The vast dome overhead is a cloudless azure and thousands of blue and white icebergs drift by in stately procession from the glacier at the head of the bay. The scene is matchless – incomparable. Slowly, lingeringly, the sun swoons in the western sea and "departing rays sent from afar across mysterious mirrors" touch the mountain peaks, gilding their snowy whiteness. The canopy of blue is now a mass of brilliant crimson and gold that constantly shifts and changes form and shape like the fragments of glass in a kaleidoscope. Gradually the brilliancy fades, the colors grow faint, fainter, and drowsy night begins to kindle her starry lamps.

* *

There are many interesting coast towns in Alaska. Juneau, the capital, clings to the side of a beetling mountain. It has a population of 2,500 and is modern in every respect. Just across from Juneau is Douglas Island on which are located the largest quartz mines in the world.

Cordova, away over on the southwestern coast, is the terminus of the Copper River Railroad. This is one of the newest but most progressive of modern Alaska towns.

Valdez is the town where "sails meet the trails." Valdez is the most northerly open winter port in Alaska. Stages operate

Juneau, Douglas Island and Gastineau Channel, Alaska.
View of city. ca. 1900-1930. Photograph. Lib. of Cong. Washington, D.C. *Lib. of Cong.* Web. Nov. 27, 2019. <https://www.loc.gov/pictures/item/99614827/>.

Juneau, Alaska, and the surrounding mountain range.
View of city, mountains and cabelship (sic) "Burnside" in channel. ca. 1900-1930. Photograph. Lib. of Cong. Washington, D.C. *Lib. of Cong.* Web. Nov. 27, 2019. <https://www.loc.gov/pictures/item/99614828/>.

from here to Fairbanks and thence down the Yukon by dog teams. It is the supply source and starting point for miners.

Seward, still farther west, is the terminus of the Alaskan Central railway which has fifty-two miles of road finished. Three-fourths of the newspaper party stopped over in Seward three days while the Northwestern steamed across the channel to Port Graham on the western point of Kenai peninsula. Somebody had hinted that the crossing would be rough and a hint was all that was necessary to cause the wholesale exodus. However, the trip across was smooth and pleasant and the day at Port Graham, the finest of the entire trip.

There is nothing at Port Graham but a general store, the wharf buildings and one residence, but it is an important station for it is the supply point for small steamers operating on Cook Inlet and carrying supplies up the rivers into the interior. August third, the day spent at Port Graham, was an ideal one – warm as a Long Beach June.

Valdez, Alaska, in the early 1900s.
Hegg, Eric A. *Street scene*. ca. 1906-1915. Photograph. Lib. of Cong. Washington, D.C. *Lib. of Cong.* Web. Nov. 27, 2019. <https://www.loc.gov/pictures/item/99614944/>.

Seward, Alaska, from the bridge in the early 1900s.
View of Seward from bridge. ca. 1900-1930. Photograph. Lib. of Cong. Washington, D.C. *Lib. of Cong.* Web. Nov. 27, 2019. <https://www.loc.gov/pictures/item/99614572/>.

The sea was as smooth as the mill pond you used to swim in back in Illinois, the surf, a narrow strip of foamy lace, stretched lazily and noiselessly on the pebbly beach; the dense woods on the mountain side beckoned alluringly and the California bunch with the Chief in tow spent several happy hours browsing about on the native heath of the moose and bear. The sun, glancing through the wooded aisles, wove fantastic patterns of enchantment; the moss-covered earth sank under the feet like a velvet rug; gleaming pink salmonberries intermingling with green bracken and slender fern made a picture so fairy-like that one instinctively peered about for the tiny creatures.

There was something majestic in the all-pervading, solemn hush of the woods and when through a break in the thick screen of forest, a glimpse was given of a broad expanse of sea, rippling and sparkling in the sunlight; of the magnificent mountain peaks clothed in glistening raiment, one thought – as Orno Strong of Portland expressed it – of the city of the New Jerusalem which St. John described so vividly in the book of the Revelation. It seemed very near to nature's heart away off there in the quiet solemnity of that isolated spot. Cowper said, "God made the country and man made the town," and, truly, God seems more manifest in the silent places than in the busy man-made metropolis. His voice is heard in the rush of the waves, in the whisper of the wind. His presence is felt in the dim groves of trees – His first temples – and everywhere the evidences of His work.

Valdez at the head of Port Valdez, Alaska, in 1915.
Sheelor, F.W. *Valdez, Alaska, 1915*. 1915. Photograph. Lib. of Cong. Washington, D.C. *Lib. of Cong.* Web. Nov. 27, 2019. <https://www.loc.gov/pictures/item/2007661316/>.

With so little that is artificial and so much that is natural, is it strange that one feels nearer the sublime Creator of all things than in the busy marts of trade where the golden rule is, "Do others or they will do you?" Although Port Graham was established only a year ago, already customs of the outside world are creeping in and in a few months this Primeval wilderness, untainted by the tide of outing travel – this restful spot, beautiful enough to inspire dreams, poetry or painting – will be a hustling, bustling center of commercial activity.

While water fowl abound near the Alaskan coast town, few song birds such as California has so abundantly were heard. However, it is a well-known fact that in the interior there are numerous songsters. To convince skeptical passengers the Chief told a story of a Miss Elizabeth Bird who lived near Valdez. It seems that Miss Bird started early in life to feather her nest well and her first adventure outside of the home nest was when she married Bud Martin. Martin soon died and she married Edward Crow. When the time came to change nests again, she allied herself with William Robin and lived happily until the matrimonial season rolled around again for Mrs. Robin. This time Dave Buzzard, a widower, more attractive personally than his name would indicate, appeared, and she became Mrs. Buzzard. Into the buzzard roost Mrs. Buzzard carried one little Martin, two little Crows and one little Robin. One little Buzzard was already there to welcome the other birds. No doubt when her earthly career is ended, she will become a Bird of Paradise.

* *

Three thousand miles from Long Beach, which spells HOME for the Quiet One and so many that she loves – and not a letter, not a line, not a suspicion of a word in fifteen days – and the stupid boat steadily forging, hour by hour, farther north and west. She disgraces herself by crying childishly one morning, in full view of the Marathon racers as they paced their daily mile around the deck. But she did not care how many eyes regarded her – some curiously, some sympathetically, some understandingly – she just crouched down in her deck chair and shed weak, miserable tears and wanted awfully to howl. Seasickness is awful, but oh, you homesickness!

* *

Each morning as the Northwestern proceeded northward there was a frostier tang in the air and on foggy or rainy days the decks were almost deserted and the company hugged the steam pipes in the deck house. Ever encounter a fog at sea? It's nasty. Sometimes it slowly envelopes the ship – enshrouding, impenetrable. Again, it falls like a pall in less time than it takes to describe it. The mysterious depths of the greyness causes the spirits of the passengers to grow as bleak as the air that smothers, as it enfolds. The hoarse fog horn bellows out its protesting blasts and out of the dim obscurity the warning notes of a bell buoy ring out dolefully. But, have you ever, after a day that was dark and cold and dreary, felt a warm wind spring up from the south with a promise of spring? Just so one feels, when, little by little, the damp, gray, smothery substance recedes until it finally rises like a great curtain.

* *

On the homeward trip the Northwestern stopped at Metlakatla, that unique settlement made up of natives under the leadership of the venerable Father Duncan[1], a missionary who has devoted his life to work among the Indians. There are about 850 Christian Indians in the settlement. They are of the Tsimpsheau tribe.[2]

Missionary William Duncan at the Metlakatla town library.
Father William Duncan, a missionary, in front of town library. ca. 1900-1923. Photograph. Lib. of Cong. Washington, D.C. *Lib. of Cong*. Web. Nov. 27, 2019. <https://www.loc.gov/pictures/item/99614963/>.

---

1 William Duncan was an English-born Anglican missionary who founded the Tsimshian communities of Metlakatla, British Columbia, in Canada, and Metlakatla, Alaska, in the United States. Although sometimes referred to as "Father Duncan" in subsequent reports, he was never ordained.

2 The Tsimshian are an indigenous people of the Pacific Northwest Coast. Their communities are mostly in coastal British Columbia and far southern Alaska, around Terrace and Prince Rupert in British Columbia, and Alaska's Annette Islands.

Metlakatla, British Columbia, School Building in 1915.
Curtis & Miller, Seattle. *Government school building.* March 19, 1915. Photograph. Lib. of Cong. Washington, D.C. *Lib. of Cong.* Web. Nov. 27, 2019. <https://www.loc.gov/pictures/item/99614818/>.

Father Duncan has established an industrial training school, stores, saw mill, salmon cannery, library, all of which are owned and operated exclusively by Indians. There is a large cathedral with a pipe organ. A definite municipal system of government obtains, but Father Duncan is instructor and overseer as well as schoolmaster and pastor. The settlement is extremely interesting as an example of successful sociological experiment and from the fact that what was formerly a savage horde is now a Christian community. The Indian women at Metlakatla weave curious baskets and many were sold to the Northwestern's passengers.

* *

There is a subtle illusive, intangible something that grips the heart of the visitor to Alaska. It is the same "something" that holds the settler there and makes him dissatisfied with any other place of abode. It may be the larger, freer life; it may be the electricity in the atmosphere; it may be the frosts that send the blood tingling through the veins, and it may be the scenic beauty. Someone has written of the "pale, anemic sentiment of the dweller under the Polar Star," but that phase of character was not evident in Alaska. On the contrary, the people look as though sublime isolation and weathering storms had brought strength, endurance and a happy heart. The men appear to have red corpuscles and the women are beautiful – complexions like peaches and cream and with a wholesome healthfulness that always attracts.

* *

The newspaper people in their Alaskan tour covered a total of 4,272 miles from Seattle. In that long journey they read, as it were, a brief index to Alaska. They could only guess from what they saw, of the tremendous forces which are now transforming the vast Northwest into a mighty commercial empire. As eminently pleasing as the journey was from every point of view, every passenger was glad when the Northwestern docked at Seattle and there was a great scurrying for homeward-bound trains. After all, there's no place like home, especially if home is Long Beach.

"Here's to the home – a man's Kingdom, a child's paradise and a woman's world."

ALASKA OPENS EDITORS' EYES

(By United Press)

SEATTLE, Wash. Aug. 13—The members of the National Editorial Association who made the trip to Cordova, Valdez and Juneau on the steamer Northwestern returned last night. The members of the party were enthusiastic over the trip north and the climate, beauty and resources of the country was a revelation to most of the editors on board.

Tour returns to Seattle.
"Alaska Opens Editors' Eyes." The Daily Alaskan, [Skagway, Alaska] Aug. 13, 1909. *Lib. of Cong.* Web. Nov. 29, 2019. <https://chroniclingamerica.loc.gov/lccn/sn82014189/1909-08-13/ed-1/seq-1/>.

Appendix

Editors Say Alaska Is a Great Country

With a party of 134 members of the National Editorial Association, who had completed an excursion of 4,000 miles to Southwestern Alaska, as far as Port Graham and return, the Alaska Steamship Company's liner Northwestern, Capt. A. Croskey, arrived shortly after 10 o'clock Thursday night. The Alaska trip, arranged through the Seattle Press Club, concluded the annual convention, business sessions of which were held in Seattle late in July.

Speaking the declared sentiment of every member of the editorial party, B. B. Herbert, editor of the Printer-Journalist, of Chicago, founder and first president of the national organization of editors, said upon landing: "Most of us went to Alaska for the purpose of sympathizing with the residents of that Northern region over the hardships imagined in their existence. Returning, we are positive that the country presents possibilities not excelled on earth.

"We found at Seward a half-acre garden from which a Scotchman had this season sold $800 worth of vegetables. At Ketchikan, we saw them taking fish in such quantities that the canneries were turning out enough to insure great revenue. We inspected the Treadwell mines, on Douglas Island, where on the 1,400-foot level, the rich mineral deposits grow steadily more valuable; we saw gold and coal mines being developed with a sureness that is convincing to us all that without other advantages an empire of wealth is available in Alaska.

"Coupled with the many commercial surprises met in Alaska, we were regaled with a voyage so magnificent with scenic features and nature's marvels that the attention of the world must surely be attracted there as a new wonderland. No feature has been more pleasant than the splendid courtesy extended by Capt. Croskey and his officers, and the generous hospitality extended by citizens of every community visited."

Supporting the statement of former President Herbert, Secretary W.F. Parrott, of the Waterloo Daily Reporter, spoke enthusiastically of the enjoyment that had marked every hour of the voyage. He predicts for Alaska, through its coal, gold and copper, fish and wood pulp, a future as one of the greatest countries in the world.

Editors Return from Alaska.
The San Juan Islander. (Friday Harbor, Wash.), 20 Aug. 1909. Chronicling America: Historic American Newspapers. Lib. of Congress. <https://chroniclingamerica.loc.gov/lccn/sn88085190/1909-08-20/ed-1/seq-2/>

A Trip to Alaska and the Pacific Northwest

On Saturday morning, July 24th, promptly at 9 o'clock, according to previous announcement, we were all on board the good steamer Northwestern, which was to be our home for the next twenty days, during which time we would tour the lands to the north and for the first time, for many of us, if not all, look upon Uncle Sam's "better half" – Alaska. "We were crowded in the cabin" – and we were crowded in every other old place but that did not matter so long as we were at last on our long-looked-forward-to trip to Alaska. The Northwestern was a very well-appointed vessel, and one of the best and largest ships that made the northern trip. It was manned with a very efficient and accommodating set of officers whose greatest pleasure seemed to be in looking after the welfare of their party. From the very outset everything pointed to a pleasant journey and throughout the entire twenty days nothing transpired to mar the pleasure of the occasion.

The passengers, some two-hundred in number, were all cultured and refined and it would have been a hard matter indeed to find a more congenial party with which to spend a three-week's outing. The greatest good feeling prevailed and cheery greetings and peals of laughter were heard on every hand. Not a discordant word or deed occurred to mar the pleasure of the voyage. This, together with the ideal weather enabled us to start out upon our long voyage with light hearts and full of hope and expectations. As the whistle blew and we steamed from dock, a large crowd bid us God-speed and a safe journey, and as long as we were in sight, handkerchiefs fluttered in the breeze and more than once went up to the eyes to snatch away the telltale tear for, while we were on a mission of pleasure and sight-seeing, yet, we realized that we were turning our back on home and friends, and for three long weeks, would be practically without communication. 'Tis true, our ship was equipped with the Wireless Telegraph, but few of us could afford the luxury of aerograms. However, while we got no personal news yet, we were kept informed as to the leading events of the world by means of the "Wireless Daily Tribune," a little paper which "Sparks" the wireless operator, issued each day by means of a typewriter and carbon paper and which gave us the news as he received it over the Wireless Telegraph. This served wonderfully to relieve our anxiety for while we got no direct news from our homes, yet the general news told us that no dire calamities had befallen any section. In connection with the wireless news, an editorial staff was appointed from among our party and each day much fun and humor was injected into the columns of the Tribune at the expense of some member of the party. The paper found a ready sale at 5 cents a copy. The youngsters of the party served as "Newsies."

Upon entering my stateroom shortly after leaving dock, I spied an innocent looking little metallic box attached to the side of each berth. The box was about large enough to contain one

The Beaver Herald story covers the writer's trip from Oklahoma to Seattle and the cruise to Alaska. This excerpt covers the Alaska cruise.

The Beaver Herald. (Beaver, O.T. [Okla.]), Sept., 23, 1909 through Oct. 28, 1909. Chronicling America: Historic American Newspapers. Lib. of Congress. <https://chroniclingamerica.loc.gov/lccn/sn93066071/1909-09-23/ed-1/seq-8/>, <https://chroniclingamerica.loc.gov/lccn/sn93066071/1909-10-07/ed-1/seq-5/>, <https://chroniclingamerica.loc.gov/lccn/sn93066071/1909-10-14/ed-1/seq-5/>, <https://chroniclingamerica.loc.gov/lccn/sn93066071/1909-10-28/ed-1/seq-5/>.

day's well-masticated food and it didn't take me long to figure out what it had been placed there for. I had a hard time persuading myself not to get seasick on the spot, although we were on a perfectly smooth sea. But that box! It was too suggestive. I got it out of sight in a jiffy. However, after we had been out two days, we reached Queen Charlotte Sound and experienced our first rough sea. Say, that box came in handy there, alright. There was a great "uprising" on that ship, everybody seemed to be playing Jonah and fed the fish. I have been asked to describe how you feel when seasick. My best explanation is this: At first you are so sick you are afraid you will die. After a while you are so sick you are afraid you won't die. But, after all, it's mighty funny to see the other fellow. I experienced rough seas about four or five times and each time a goodly number of our party directed their attention to feeding the fish.

Our longest rough-water experience was about thirty-six hours in duration. During this time, the docks were depopulated. Most everybody stayed in their berths, for it had been noised about that the best preventive of seasickness was to lie flat on your back in bed. With the ship pitching like an Oklahoma bronco and rolling from side to side, the rails nearly dipping water, both at the same time, lying flat on the back was no joke and I found myself too sick to stay in bed and too sick to get up. Those 30 hours remain fresh in my memory. Even now I can almost feel a lump rise in my throat as I write about it. Be that as it may, the trip was well worth this slight unpleasantness and, in fact, even the sea sickness had its beneficial effects, and after it was past one felt better for the experience.

The voyage was not devoid of social functions by any means. Society was at its height and every night while on board the time was passed pleasantly in some social manner. Entertainments consisted of parties of various kinds, games, debates, mock trials, musicales, receptions, and banquets. Each Sunday was observed, both morning and evening by religious services, for beside the editors, we had two ministers and a number of W.C.T.U. workers in the party as well as Y.W.C.A. and Anti-Saloon League leaders.

Our first step In Alaska was made at Ketchikan, two days' travel from Seattle, at a good little town of 1,500 inhabitants which nestled against the mountainside and extended out over the waters of the bay. This was a boardwalk town. The streets as well as the sidewalks were made of heavy planks. Through the cracks one could see the clear water of the bay sparkling beneath. Almost the entire town was built on piling. Ketchikan is the first American port of entry. The custom house is located here. Here we received our first surprise as to the manner and customs of Alaska. When the name "Alaska" is first brought to our attention, our mind at once reverts to thoughts of snow and ice and fur-clad people. It was with some-such anticipation as this, that most of us were expecting to see, when we made our first landing. We had been traveling within sight of snow-clad mountains all along, and the chilling breezes spoke in no uncertain tones, of ice and snow. Imagine then our surprise when our good ship steamed up to dock and we set our foot again on American soil – no, I mean planks, for I have told you this city is built over the water – and made our way around the town, to find everything just as lovely and pleasant, and far more picturesque, than in most portions of the states.

Window boxes contained pansies, nasturtiums, and other flowers and plants, growing and blooming in the greatest profusion, and a gentle Italian Zephyr was stirring the leaves of the many varieties of beautiful ferns and trees, all of which were growing wild in the greatest luxuriance. Many varieties of berries were found which yielded abundantly and the fruit was large and delicious. The Salmonberry, so called on account of its color, is among those that grow most profusely. This berry resembles the blackberry and is very delicious. The wild berries are equal in every way to the tame ones raised in the states, and are used for canning, preserving, jams and jellies.

In speaking of berries, we learned at Ketchikan that not a poisonous berry plant, vine, insect, or reptile is known to exist in Alaska. In all its wide borders, not a snake or poisonous insect abounds, and one is perfectly safe in eating any berry or fruit they may find growing without fear of harm.

The city is noted for its water supply. Pipes are run directly from the falls of the Ketchikan River supplying the citizens with ice-cold, refreshing water from this pure mountain stream. It is said to be the best system in Alaska.

Our visit to Ketchikan gives us our first foundation for a fish story which we defy anyone to excel. The sight which greeted our eyes here was truly marvelous, but so often was it repeated at our various stops, that along with the other wonders it became commonplace. In our walk about Ketchikan, the numerous citizens with which we conversed would remark in every instance, "Have you been down to see the fish?" So often was this question asked that we were convinced "the fish" must be the thing to see, so we followed the crowd.

Arriving at the shallower water of the bay, a bridge had been constructed across one arm of the same, and upon approaching the spot, we noted the whole face of the water in motion, and bright shining objects flashing in the sunlight above the water. Closer examination disclosed that the bay was filled with millions of salmon, and the continual splash, splash, of the fish as they jumped from one to two foot out of the water, coming down broadside, beat anything I ever saw. This was during spawning season, and the fish were not good for canning, but the fishermen made a haul anyway for our benefit, and at one drag, which took less than twenty minutes, they secured a row-boat full of salmon. As we stood on the bridge and watched the schools of fish pass, the water looked like one squirming mass and so thick were the salmon that the sandy bottom of the bay could not be seen. Now I know, dear readers, that this sounds like a pretty big fish story, but those were big fish, and I can refer you to some two-hundred editors who can verify all I have said.

Here, we saw the house of the chief of the Thlingit Indians and the famous Kyam totem pole which stands before it. Another remarkable thing was the tombstones which stood before the houses of the Indians. We inquired if the dead were interred there and were informed that they were not, but that the cemetery or burying-ground was on an adjacent island and the stones erected at the residence. These stones were merely set on the walk, and as the planks sprung in passing, the grave sentinels would tip and totter accordingly.

Many persons are unfamiliar with the Indian history of Alaska and a great deal of mystery has been thrown around the numerous totem columns in the Native villages along the southeastern coast of Uncle Sam's new district. These pictographic carvings are a source of interest to tourists visiting the north, and are not idols as might be supposed, but in a general way, may be said to be family registers.

Ages ago, the Indians adopted totems, or crests, to distinguish the four social clans into which the race is said to be divided. The names of these clans in the Tsimshian language are the

Kishpootwadda, Lacheboo, Canadda and Lackshkeak. The Kishpootwadda's are more numerous in Alaska and are represented symbolically by the finback whale in the sea, the grizzly bear on land, the grouse in the air, and the sun and stars in the heavens. The Canadda symbols are the frog, raven, starfish, and bullhead. The Lacheboo took the wolf, heron, and the grizzly bear for their totems, while the Lackshkeaks have the eagle, beaver, and the halibut.

The creatures are regarded by the Indians as the representatives of the powerful and mythical beings of the Native mythology. As all of any one of the groups are said to be of the same kindred, members of a clan whose heraldic symbols are identical, are counted as blood relations. Strange as it may seem, this relationship holds good should the persons belonging to different or hostile tribes, speak a different language, or be located thousands of miles apart.

The Indians on being asked to explain how this notion of relationship originated, point back to a remote age when their ancestors lived in a most beautiful land. It was then that the mythical creatures, whose symbol they still retain, revealed themselves to the heads of the families of that day.

Many of the Alaska Indians still relate a traditional story of a flood which came and submerged the land, spreading death and destruction everywhere. Those who escaped in their canoes drifted about, and scattered in every direction. When the flood subsided, they settled on the land where their boats rested and formed new tribal associations.

Thus it was, that persons related by blood, became widely separated. They still clung, however, to the symbols which had distinguished them and their families. To the present day, the Alaska Indians have sacredly followed the old customs. The crests continue to mark the offspring of the original founders of the family. It is the ambition of all leading members of each clan in the several tribes to represent their symbols of heraldry by carving or painting on all their belongings. Upon the death of the head of a family, a totem pole is erected in front of the house of the successor on which is generally carved the symbolic creatures of the dead Indian's clan. The crests also define the bonds on consanguinity and persons having the same crest are forbidden to intermarry.

A frog may not marry a frog, or a whale a whale, but a frog may marry a wolf, and a whale may be united in marriage to an eagle. Among some tribes in Alaska, the marriage restrictions are still further narrowed and persons of different crests do not intermarry if the creatures of their clans have the same instincts.

That is, a Canadda may not marry a Lackshkeak because the raven of one crest and the eagle of the other seek to devour the same kind of food. The Kishpootwadda may not marry a Lacheboo since the grizzly bear and the wolf, representing those crests, are both carnivorous.

All Indian children take the crest of their mother. They do not regard their father's family as their relations. Therefore, a man's heir or successor is not his own son, but his sister's son. The clan relationship also has a great deal to do with promoting hospitality among the Indians, which is a matter of immense importance.

Having spent our allotted time at Ketchikan viewing the wonderful totem poles, salmon fisheries, and magnificent scenery in general, we again boarded the "Northwestern" to resume our journey to the wonderful northland, and with every forward movement of the mighty ship, new scenes were brought into our view. In our journey so far, we had sailed along the inside passage, steaming in and out among the many beautiful islands, at times coming so close to shore that it seemed we might almost reach out our hands and pluck a flower or fern with which the entire surface of the land was so gorgeously arrayed. For wonder and splendor, the islands could not be surpassed by the far-famed Thousand Islands of the St. Lawrence themselves.

But, after leaving Ketchikan, the scene was changed. Snow-capped mountains rearing their lofty peaks far above the horizon were to be seen on every hand and the valleys and canons intervening were filled with immense glaciers. As we first looked upon the scene, it appeared as if a mighty river was rushing madly down the mountain side, but upon closer inspection through the field glass, we were convinced that we had reached the land of glaciers and icebergs, and before the day had passed, we had actually experienced all the thrills of sailing right among the wonderful things themselves.

As we sailed up Taku Inlet, we got our first real view of the icebergs. Some of the "early birds" gave the alarm that they had sighted an iceberg and it was not long before the deck was lined with eager sight-seers anxious to get a first look. How we did marvel at the beauty of the floating ice. We thought we had seen the real thing when we looked at those small pieces of ice and called it an iceberg. Had our vessel right-about-faced right there, we would have come home fully convinced that we had seen the frozen icebergs of the frozen north in all their grandeur.

As it was, we had only just begun to taste of the real pleasures of our visit. Our good ship steamed along at a good rate and the floating ice became more numerous and much larger. Every once in a while, we would pass within only a short distance of a berg and a shout of delight would go up from all, but imagine our surprise when we took time to look ahead and saw that we were headed straight toward a whole "swarm" of icebergs, many of them half as large as our vessel itself, and in such close proximity that it seemed almost impossible for us to sail any further among them. Looking a little farther ahead, we saw the marvelous Taku Glacier from which the bergs were being constantly sent tumbling into the sea, sending the silvery foam surging high up the wall-like cliffs. Still our ship pressed onward.

Two pilots with eagle-eyes walked the upper deck, and one stood at the helm to steer our craft through safely and we crept along at a snail-like pace, the bow of the ship pushing the smaller burgs aside and fairly grating against the sides of the larger ones. Every officer and every boatswain was at his post of duty, and every knot of progress was made with the utmost caution, for navigation was extremely dangerous and if we missed our course, it meant disaster. We were all too much enchanted with the beauty and grandeur of the scene to realize fully just to what an extent we were taking our lives in our own hands to satisfy our curiosity to see, but now and then when it seemed our boat would surely strike against one of the huge islands of ice, even the bravest hearted would forget the beautiful and a thrill of fear would almost cause them to turn pale and tremble.

When we had advanced as far as it was deemed advisable by the Captain, and much farther than your humble servant cared about going, we dropped anchor and remained for a few minutes until all had an opportunity of seeing the mighty glacier and the Kodac-fiends had snapped some of the beauty to carry home with them. Then we beat our retreat and when we were in clear water again, we all took a good breath and sat down to ponder and talk over the sights we had seen.

From this time on, icebergs and glaciers were no uncommon sight. We had them nearly all the way along. At times as many as twelve or fifteen glaciers could be counted within full view of the deck. If ever words failed to express the beauty and charm of nature, it is when we come to tell of those things of which we have just been writing. I wish I were an artist and could paint you the picture, not leaving out a single sparkle, gleam, or hue. What a picture it would be, indeed. All shades of green, red, topaz, blue, in fact, every shade of the rainbow is blended with perfect harmony in the ice, and seems studded with diamonds and rubies which sparkle and dance in the light.

Climatic conditions, taken all together, are favorable for the growth of glaciers in Alaska. A recent writer says "that true glaciers are confined to the southern parts of the territory and depend on the combinations of climatic and topographical conditions for their extent and geographical distribution." All glaciers are formed in regions of perpetual snow, but recent explorations show that not all perpetual snow mountains contain these vast ice-beds. When glacial ice is absent in the valleys of snow-covered ranges, it is because other necessary conditions are lacking. No matter how many other arms or branches a glacier may have spread in traverse valleys intersecting the main glacial valley, all are connected with the perpetual snow-caps above.

Great humidity, which causes abundant snow-fall, is one of the conditions that must be present for the formation of glaciers on the heights. To compact the millions of tiny crystals into glacier ice, the snow must be subjected to a changeable temperature, alternate thawing and freezing. Many persons probably wonder why these great white fields extend below the snow line, and below the mean line of 32 degrees, or freezing point. A brief explanation is given by the late Professor Joseph Le Conte in the following words: "The upper part of a glacier is perpetual snow, which has drifted in and fills the summit valley. Lower down the valley, one finds a granulated or intermediate snow, that is, a formation between snow and ice which gradually changes to glacier ice in the lower altitudes." By the gravitation and pressure of the upper ice fields, the face of the glacier moves snail-like to tide water where weather conditions cause the great chunks to break away from the active glacier and float about in navigable waters.

Nearly all glaciers of Alaska are prolongations of vast ice fields fed from the tops of high and stately peaks. The glaciers are moving all the time, but only very slowly, and the glacial ice freed by coming in contact with the sea usually finds an outlet to the Pacific through one of the many fjords, and the action of the warm ocean current causes these broken masses to melt away. The borders of many of Alaska's glaciers are moraine-covered and contain small and shallow lakes. The formation seems to be initiated by the melting back of the sides of crevasses, as they broaden the openings are filled with water and miniature rivers flow here and there on the slopes of the glacier feeding into the icy depressions.

Travelers who journey to Alaska will find that the residents have applied the term "live glaciers" to ice-fields discharging into the ocean. Those located on the mountain slopes far above sea level are generally referred to as glaciers of the Alpine-type because they so resemble the glacial ice of the Alps in Switzerland. Glaciers which formerly discharged into large bodies of water but are now separated by moraines are termed "dead glaciers."

Our next stop, we made at Treadwell. Here we were allowed to visit the biggest gold mine in the world. This mine is called the Glory Hole. Some of our party donned the coats and caps of the miners and made the descent into the Hole. It was a thrilling experience. We were allowed to visit all parts of the large plant and the working of the machinery and the process used in separating the gold from the quartz was a revelation to many of us.

Quite a joke was perpetrated upon a number of our party. If you have ever been in a stamping mill, you know just what they are. Nobody ever forgets a visit to such a place. Well, the word was passed around that we were going to be allowed the privilege of visiting the great stamping mill at Treadwell where two-hundred immense machines were stamping out the gold from the rocks, but if we were allowed this privilege, it would be necessary for us to keep perfectly still and no one would be allowed to speak loud enough to be heard. We all readily consented and proceeded on our way.

Before we reached the mill however, we found that we had been the victims of a huge joke, for even at that distance, so great was the noise of the mill itself, that one had fairly to shout to be understood. It is needless to say that none spoke so as to be heard when once inside the mill. These stamps are mammoth crushers which pulverize the rocks. This pulverized substance is then subjected to several processes of washing by which the gold is separated from the quartz, the gold adhering to a large cylinder, and the waste being carried on by the flow of the water.

Our visit was very interesting and it was with a great deal of reluctance that we bid the good people of Treadwell goodbye. Before sailing, a reception and banquet was tendered to the party by the owners of the mine and the citizens of Treadwell.

Juneau, the capital of Alaska, is only a short distance from Treadwell, and was our next stop. Here we were tendered a royal welcome and every moment of our stay was thoroughly enjoyed. The citizens are big-hearted and wide-awake, and although in a semi-isolated district, they know just how things ought to be done and are found doing them. Juneau is the largest business port in Alaska. It has several modern church buildings as well as a high school and court house, and its business district cannot be excelled. It is indeed marvelous to note the immense stock of goods carried by the merchants and the high quality of the same.

There is nothing shoddy in Alaska. Everything is new and up-to-date. Juneau has a Government cable and thus has connection with the outside world by telegraph. Here we found two daily papers both doing a good business. The population is about 3,000. They have complete electric, light, water works, and telephone systems, and during the summer and winter, theatrical performances are given in the Juneau opera house.

Leaving Juneau, we soon passed out into the Pacific and enjoyed for about thirty-six hours "A life on the ocean wave, a home on the rolling deep," the experiences of which I told you in a former article. It was truly a taste of real ocean-life and an experience I am sure which will remain uppermost in the minds of those who took the memorable journey. About noon the second day at sea, we "passed in" at Cape Hinchinbrook and were again upon calm sea in Prince William Sound on which waters we proceeded to Cordova.

A few hours after leaving Valdez, we found ourselves in the Alaskan whaling waters and here got our first sight of those monsters of the sea. For a long time, I had noticed the water being spouted high in the air much resembling the action of the sand in a Beaver County whirlwind and I was beginning to wonder if I really was going to see anything like beaver way up in the waters of the Alaskan Pacific, when I heard someone shout, "See the whale!" Of course, I was all eyes for if I missed anything on that trip, it was when I was seasick. We were all missing much then – however I found that it was only the "spouts" which I had been seeing all the time that they had sighted. As we watched, now and then we could get a glimpse through the glass of the black body of the whales as they spouted in the distance but we had not proceeded far until we got a fine view of a large whale real close to our ship. The officers or our ship told us that this whale was a fine specimen and one of the largest of those waters.

Later we saw a number of whales and numerous porpoises and seals. Albatross and sea gulls were in great abundance as well as sea parrots and other birds, the names of which we failed to learn. It was on our trip from Valdez to Seward that we had our longest ocean ride. We were in the open ocean thirty-six hours on this trip. Many, in fact most all, experienced serious seasickness, but everybody kept sweet – and if they couldn't laugh, they would at least smile.

It was on this voyage that many of our most beautiful mountain scenes were to be seen. We passed the Fairweather Range whose lofty peaks rose high toward heaven and above the clouds. Two peaks of this range in particular, seemed to stand side by side, and their snow-covered peaks seemed to puncture the sky so towering was their height. Mt. McKinley, 20,300 feet and the highest mountain north of Mexico, was discernable, as well as Mt. St. Elias, 18,024 feet, Mt. Logan, 10,640 feet, and a number of others. Mt. St. Elias is the corner-post of the international boundary line between the United States and Canada, where the boundary starts and follows the 141st meridian direct to the Arctic Ocean. Around Mt. St. Elias, clings the romance of discovery, as it was the first land sighted by Bering, July 10, 1741. A few of the Alaska mountains are crowned with fire and snow. Mt. Wrangell is the most southerly of the volcanic mountains. It is not an active volcano but smoke is frequently seen issuing from its craters.

When we landed at Seward, we had reached our northern terminus, and when we set sail again, it would be to turn our faces in the direction of home. 'Tis true our ship went on to Port Graham, on Cook's Inlet, but as this was only a trading post with nothing of interest to be seen, most of our party remained at Seward to take in the scenes of that beautiful country and to rest up somewhat for the return trip. At Seward we found another railroad, the Alaskan Central, and were the guests of the company on a trip out to the end of the line, some fifty miles. Everything was arranged for our convenience and lunch was prepared for the mid-day meal. This was a wonderful trip. The scenery was unsurpassed and was varied to the extreme.

Leaving Seward, we passed over a long stretch of level country and actually found vegetation existing as in the states. "The ranch" was pointed out to us as we passed, and of course I looked at once for the cattle for that is what we have on Beaver County ranches, but I found instead that they said "ranch" when in reality they meant "farm," for before us real farm life presented itself. Potatoes, corn, and various other garden products were growing luxuriantly as well as grain and other farm products.

After a time, we entered the mountains and here the real beauty of the ride was to be seen. The scene was constantly changing and each time it seemed more enchanting. Now we were passing through a dense forest with no way to look but straight up and again we were in the open making our way along the bank of some beautiful stream or mountain lake. One of the prettiest scenes of the trip was that presented by Mirror Lake. As the name implies the lake is a most perfect mirror. The surface of the water was placid and mirrored in its depths were the snow caps of the surrounding mountains and the wooded sides which were plainly depicted in the water. A Kodak picture of the scene was so perfect that it was hard indeed to tell the reflection from the real object.

This trip gave us a glimpse of wildlife in Alaska. We had seen about everything that was to be seen in the sea as well as on land but we had not yet had a view of any of Alaska's wild animals of which we had heard so much. This trip furnished us that feature and completed our category. A peculiar shriek of the engine warned us that something unusual had happened and the train came to a dead stop. The keen-sighted engineer had sighted a moose and he, together with the fireman donning their rubber hip-boots, made their way into the jungle and scared out the animal. The moose was most accommodating running out in a clear spot where with head erect, he stopped, and with right-about-face, stood as if posing for the many Kodak's that were pointed his way, and then run on, and was lost in the wilds and wood again. Some of our party humorously accused the good citizens of Seward of having borrowed someone's pet moose for this occasion and complimented the owner upon the good behavior of his mooseship. Be that as it may, we saw the moose alright.

The roadbed of the Alaska Central passes directly through a "dead" glacier, and at this point our accommodating trainmen again stopped and allowed us to satisfy our curiosity and our desires to set foot upon one of those frozen rivers. A short distance ahead, we found snow and all indulged in a free-for-all snowball fight. A peculiar scene presented itself, just here, for while we were standing on one side of the track snow-balling, others were at the other side gathering as beautiful flowers as were ever seen. No one was able to account for the snow being there, and the flowers as well, but there they were, whether they could be accounted for or not.

Dinner was served on the return trip at a beautiful spot where grass and flowers were growing profusely and where the sun shone down with such force that we were almost compelled to hunt a shade. We stopped at the flower beds on our return and went home with our train loaded down with a wealth of beauty which could not be excelled even by the famed flowers of Colorado.

During our stay of two days in Seward, we were royally treated and the enterprising citizens left nothing undone that could be done for the entertainment of their guests and even though we knew that we were to start upon our return to home and friends from this point, it was with reluctance that we sighted the Northwestern heave in sight from Port Graham, for her arrival marked the close of our visit with the good people of that place. Our return trip covered much of the same ground that we had traversed in going except that we made the trip so as to pass in the day what places we had passed in the night in going. However, there was not much night in Alaska. The daylight period beginning at 3 o'clock a.m., and closing about 11:30 p.m., it was not uncommon sight to see passengers seated about the vessel at 11 o'clock p.m. reading without an artificial light.

Various stops were made on the return trip, the most interesting of which was at Metlakatla, a quaint Indian settlement established by "Father" Duncan, a Scotch missionary, who has been among the Indians and Christianizing them for the past fifty years. Mr. Duncan is now

72 years "young" as he states it, and has done wonderful work among the Indians. About one-thousand Indians are located here who have been civilized and educated through the efforts of Father Duncan alone. No other white man is allowed to reside on the island on which Metlakatla is located, it being especially set apart by the government of the United States for the use of Mr. Duncan in his missionary work. His followers are neatly dressed and devout. They have built comfortable homes, a school house, and a large church after the style of Westminster Abbey, in which is to be found the only pipe organ in Alaska. They also own and operate a saw-mill and salmon cannery. Everything in the town is owned by Father Duncan and his Indians, and the greatest goodwill and harmony prevails.

Metlakatla was our last stop on our return home. On Friday, the thirteenth day of August, we arrived at port in Seattle, and the 24th annual convention and excursion of the National Editorial Association was at a close.

THE END.

Description of Trip Through Alaska Enjoyed by Editors
Twenty Days Delightfully Spent by National Editors
in One of the United State's Wealthiest Possessions

The Senior Editor of The Commonwealth, accompanied by his wife, recently visited the wonderland of Alaska, being with a party composed of 134 members of the National Editorial Association, which held its 44th annual session at Seattle, July 19th to 23rd 1909, a brief account of which was printed in the last issue of this paper.

On the morning of Saturday, July 24th, we boarded the Alaska Steamship Company's good steamer, "Northwestern," a splendidly appointed and commodious vessel, 330 feet long, with a displacement of 4,400 tons.

There were on board 204 first-class passengers and about 100 in the steerage, in addition to the boat-crew of over 100. Captain Alfred Croskey, an affable gentleman and efficient navigator, who formerly had charge of the "Northwestern" when she did service between New York and the Philippine Islands for five years, was in command, assisted by a courteous and capable corps of officers and men under him.

First Stop Was Ketchikan, Alaska

The route from Seattle along the coast of British Columbia and Alaska, among the thousands of islands which outly the coast north of the Strait of Juan de Fuca, is through Active Pass, into the Gulf of Georgia, between Vancouver Island and the mainland, and thence northward for nearly five-hundred miles through foreign waters, past Dixon Entrance and along Revillagigedo Channel and Tongass Narrows, to Ketchikan, the first stop and first port in Alaska, and 662 miles north of Seattle.

The people of Ketchikan entertained us splendidly during our short stop. The mayor, editor, business men, and a band of good music welcomed us to their thriving little manufacturing and mining town of about 1,500 people.

Ketchikan occupies a place at the foot of a rocky hill, being built out on the ledge to the edge of the water. The town, in the main, is one built on piles, over the water, the flooring of the houses, the walks, and streets being some twenty

The Commonwealth editor's review of the Alaska tour.
The Commonwealth. (Greenwood, Miss.), 10 Sept. 1909. Chronicling America: Historic American Newspapers. Lib. of Congress. <https://chroniclingamerica.loc.gov/lccn/sn89065008/1909-09-10/ed-1/seq-1/>.

feet above the water. All of the houses are built of wood, so are the elevated walks and streets. In the main portions of the town, the streets and walks run at right angles, but on the outskirts, the wooden paths or bridges ramble along in all directions. There are some step slopes on several streets. How do the horses manage? We didn't see a single horse or vehicle, but were told the horse population amounted to only three.

Great Salmon Fishing

If Ketchikan is short on stock it is long on salmon. In fact, a creek which runs through the town and is inhabited by millions of salmon, in the spawning season, was the cause of the founding of the town among the rather unhospitable surroundings.

Fortunately on the day the editors were present, the salmon were entering the creek and ascending the rapids, in order that they might spawn in protected nooks. Thousands were to be seen swimming in great schools in the shallow and clear creek water. All were headed up-stream. The creek runs over rocks and there are some rapids where the water rushes down with great force. But the salmon leap up these falls, fling themselves on the rocks, and work their way upward. In the broad part of the creek, near its mouth where it debauches into the inland-channel of the sea, a half dozen fishermen in boats lowered their nets and made one haul for the benefit of the 134 editors who assembled on-shore to watch the feat.

When the salmon deposit the spawn, they die, males and females alike. The young fish who are born thrive on the decaying bodies of their parents. After they get big enough to care for themselves, the salmon go to salt water, and remain away four years, when they instinctively return to spawn and die. It is said the fish return to the same stream where they were originally spawned.

There is an extensive salmon-canning plant at Ketchikan. During the spawning season, millions of salmon are captured. The United States and the Orient furnish markets for the canned output.

The sort of salmon caught in these waters are known as "humpies," derived from a hump on the fish. When the salmon die in the creek, the water becomes filthy and the Natives declare it has too much "humpy juice."

A haul of as many as 100,500 salmon has been made at Ketchikan.

Viewing Quaint Totem Poles

Totem poles, planted by real worshippers, were seen by the editors for the first time in Ketchikan. A number of these incongruous things are in various parts of the quaint city, beaten and stained, they stand in the midst of a new civilization, a reminder of the things that have gone before.

One big totem pole that shoots up some fifty feet is surmounted by a raven. An explanation of its significance is that a raven once flew to the sea, there wedded a fish, and the union started the Indian race that worshipped at the pole.

During our stay at Ketchikan, a number of the Indian population were on the sea engaged in fishing. Not a great number of Natives were noticed in the streets of Ketchikan.

Treadwell, Douglas, and Juneau

Proceeding northward, the next stop was at Treadwell Mines, Douglas, and Juneau, which are close together. The people were very hospitable and entertained their visitors with dancing and addresses, both afternoon and evening. Juneau has 2,500 people, daily newspapers, banks, theatres, good hotels, and stores. It is the gate to Skagway and lower Yukon points. Besides the Treadwell Mine across the Sound, which has produced $35,000,000 of gold, there are other quartz properties from which equal results are anticipated.

For a thousand miles, the "Northwestern" steamed through the Inside Passage, pine-clad hills tipped with snow, towering mountains with white peaks far above the clouds, countless islands, wonderful glaciers, and beautiful cascades. One of the glaciers of Taku was visited, the Steamer approaching it closely. Once in awhile a whale was sighted, and schools of porpoises raced with the ship. Nowhere else is there any such scenery. Storms do not mar the enjoyment. The passage is narrow, the mountainous banks closing it in from the tempest on both sides, hence it is as quiet as a river. People from all over the world are beginning to come to see it. It is one of the earth's great sights. A more superb panorama could not be imagined. Lofty volcanic rock formations shoot their sheer sides hundreds of feet above the sea and enclose the brilliant-hued glacier – a rugged pack of ice, a mile in breadth, extending along the valley back for miles and forced forward constantly by the tremendous pressure from behind. Countless tons of frozen crags are precipitated into the sea and begin their journey southward.

There is superb scenery along the Taku Inlet, misty clouds veiling the snowy summits and giving a proper setting to the ice-dotted channel.

There is a second glacier in the Taku Inlet, but it is not active. It is dull-colored and has ceased to move and drop its acres of ice into the Inlet. The "active" and the "dead" glaciers are quite close together and may be viewed in a single glance.

Captain Croskey took the "Northwestern" some distance out of the regular course in order to visit the glacier, and the passage is more or less dangerous, but the Editorial party were given the best in sight. This side-trip consumed a couple of hours and after the vessel had stopped at the glacier and permitted an extended view to the tourists, she was turned around and steamed for the main channel.

The Alaskan Elks

Juneau Elks are justly proud of their new $30,000 home. It contains on the first floor bowling alleys, buffet, library, billiard room, and reception hall. On the second floor is the ball room, and the lodge rooms are above. There are 250 affiliated with the Juneau Order, and in all of Alaska there is but one other club, that at Skagway. The Juneau Club House is built of wood, the interior work being very costly.

In the evening, one of the "Northwestern's" passengers, a citizen of Cordova, was properly initiated. The Elk Editors were all present and enjoyed the evening very much.

Delightful Stop at Progressive Cordova

We started for Cordova shortly after midnight, July 29th, passing through the Icy Strait by the Muir Glacier into the open sea, a distance of a 48-hour ride, on which a number of passengers got sea sick the second day out. On the first day the weather was clear and warm and nearly all day we were in sight of a mountain panorama of indescribable grandeur and beauty. The whole country along the Alaskan coast is one continuous chain of high snow-capped mountains, ranging ordinarily from two- to seven-thousand feet high, but here there can be seen in addition, three mountains in the background reaching from ten-thousand to fourteen-thousand feet high, and rounding the landscape off with such bewildering impressive effects, that the stranger is spellbound at the wonderful sight. Later in the afternoon we got farther into the open sea and the first signs of sea sickness became evident.

The usual evening entertainment was struck off the program and most of the passengers retired quite early. The next morning found many on the sick list, but all recovered during the day and when we reached Prince William Bay everybody on board had recovered and was of good, cheerful disposition. Cordova was reached the next morning, July 31st. This town is not much over two-years old and contains probably a thousand people. It is situated on a hillside and is the starting point of the Copper River Railroad, which is completed fifty-odd-miles out in the mountains and employs at present about four-thousand men to extend the road to the copper-ore holdings owned by the company. On account of these operations, Cordova presents a lively appearance. Everybody seems to be busy, either in the mercantile business, or in putting up new buildings.

Our party was scheduled for a ride into the interior to see the country. The business men, as well as the officials of the railroad, seemed to be particularly anxious that such a trip be made, and at 9 o'clock in the morning had a special train ready at the wharf to take us out. The equipment of the train was modern in every respect, consisting of first-class day coaches and a baggage car carrying refreshments. The road runs along the coast for a short distance and then branches off into the interior, crossing the Copper River, over which there is now being built one of the strongest iron bridges in America, and terminating about a dozen miles farther on, in close proximity to two big glaciers, one the Childs, to the left, and one, the Miles, to the right. It was nearly dinner time, but we were informed that we might take a look at the Childs Glacier first.

Of course, we gladly availed ourselves of the opportunity of seeing a really big glacier so close by and rushed out of the cars to the river bank to take in the sight. But we had forgotten that we were in Alaska and that everything here had to be calculated upon a scale entirely its own. Everything is immense, be it distance, size, height, length, or breadth. To the average eye, the atmospheric conditions here are deceiving. What appears to be a big hill of six- to eight-hundred-feet high, at a distance of apparently four to five miles, looms up as a mountain from three- to five-thousand-feet high, after you have traveled at least a dozen and more miles. Here the big glacier appeared to be right at our feet and everybody ran to get there first, but they soon fell into an easy gait and not until they had traveled over a mile through underbrush and over all kinds of boulders strewn in all directions, did they reach a point of close observation.

At last they were in front of the big glacier, only a thousand feet away across the river. There it was in all its grandeur and sublimity. The sight makes an indescribable impression. In fact, but few people believe in its immensity without seeing it. Think of a perpendicular ice wall 280 feet high and many miles long and you have a picture as it was actually seen by the newspaper people. There we were, gazing at nature's wonder, moving back and forth, awestruck at a sight so enchanting and bewildering.

Every few minutes a big chunk of ice as large as the steamer "Northwestern" would break off, plunging down into the deep river below with a noise like deep rolling thunder and throwing up waves that would raise the water to a considerable extent on the other shore. Reluctantly, we parted at last from the panorama before us. Dinner was ready and there were several surprises in store for us before returning to Cordova.

Dinner was served in a large hall in which the railroad men were taking their meals. It was a spacious room and especially fitted up for the occasion, and it must be admitted that the committee in charge did themselves proud in entertaining the visitors. The menu was so elaborate and well-prepared that the guests, and particularly the ladies, loudly called for the cook, to publicly express their appreciation of his successful efforts, but the good man appeared to be too modest and could not be induced to present himself.

After dinner, the party again boarded the cars to be conveyed to the river, where they were ferried over to the other side where another train was in waiting to carry us to the other end of the line, a distance of about ten miles. The ferry boat crosses the river between the Childs and Miles Glaciers, the one on the right bank of the river and the other on the left bank. The Miles Glacier is even wider than the Childs Glacier but about fifty feet lower, also a live one, and huge chunks of ice drop off frequently and sometimes impede the course of the ferry boat. When we passed the river, a block of large dimensions had lodged right in front of the landing place and we were compelled to steam around it to effect a landing. From here, the road runs between the Copper River, with its foaming and tumultuous rapids, and massive mountains rising abruptly to dizzy heights. It is a magnificent view, strange and stirring, and well-worth the trip. Now and then we passed large tents occupied by the engineers and workmen of the road.

Soon we reached the end of the line and here we were received by the officials of the road, citizens of Cordova, and part of our own people, who had preceded us while we were viewing the Childs Glacier. Large tents were in evidence everywhere and we were at once cordially invited to partake of the hospitality of the tent city. Of course, we did not resist. There were cigars, beer, wines, champagne, and something stronger for the gentlemen, and light drinks of various kinds, including tea and coffee, for the ladies. The weather was fair, the air invigorating, and the refreshments inspiring, all conducive to happiness and good fellowship, and one of the most pleasant afternoons on our voyage was spent right here on the banks of the Copper River.

But why all this expense of an extra train and entertaining the visitors so lavishly at Cordova? Well there was an object behind it all and that was to acquaint the people in the states with the enormous resources and wealth of Alaska. We learned here that gold is looked upon as of secondary importance, and that copper, and coal, and farming in districts suitable for it, will be the making of the territory. It is quite evident that copper ore is almost inexhaustible and that high-quality coal has already been found in quantities exceeding that of the coal in the states. If this is true, which it apparently is, it can be readily seen that in the near future, Alaska is bound to become one of the richest states in the Union.

While at Cordova, we met E.W. Exum, a native of Yazoo County, Mississippi, who is connected with the stores department of the Copper River Ry.; also John L. Gattis, son of Mrs. D.B. Lott, residing near Greenwood, who is connected with the publication of the Daily Alaskan; we also met W.H. Shefler, a former citizen of Scranton, at Juneau, who is city editor of the Daily Record at that place. Each of these gentlemen seemed to be prospering, they were especially pleased to see us and made our visit very pleasant.

Enjoyable Stop at Seward

Quite a number of the editors, by special invitation, stopped at Seward until the "Northwestern" completed her trip to Port Graham. At Seward, the people were exceptionally hospitable. They showered us with excursions, balls, and luncheons galore, and each vied with the other in making our stay pleasant and agreeable. In port here were G.E. Perkins, son-in-law of J.P. Morgan, with a party of friends who had chartered and partially rebuilt the "Yucatan" for the trip. Seward has its daily paper and other evidences of faith in the future.

It also has a railroad, the Alaska Central, which has crossed the divide and is being extended to the Matanuska coal fields and Fairbanks. We were taken fifty or sixty miles over it and had a picnic lunch in a little valley with a sun so warm that we almost fancied we were back at home. This road not only passes close to the base of a large glacier but it actually cuts through two little ones, where our party got out of the cars and engaged in snow-balling for several minutes.

Rich quartz discoveries are also being made just back of Seward, and the vast coal fields, which will be developed by the completion of the railroad, guarantees a prosperous future for Seward. At Seward, we met some splendid gentlemen, among the number being Mr. Hawkins, a leading banker and merchant, and Mr. Frank Watson, a wealthy coal- and gold-mine owner. Both are native Virginians, and we were under special obligations for the royal- and whole-souled entertainment and many courtesies shown us. Among other things, they gave a dozen of us a sumptuous dinner party and a 25-mile midnight excursion on a gasoline car over the Alaska Central Railway, giving us the novel and superb view of the snow-covered mountains and beautiful rivers and lakes en-route. We had to wear heavy over-coats on this trip and arrived back to Seward at 3:30 a.m., just as the sun was rising. Here the sun sets at about 10 p.m. and rises at about 3:30 a.m. The thermometer registered from 35 to 50 degrees above zero at that season of the year.

Port Graham, End of Trip

Port Graham, the end of the "Northwestern's" trip, is on Cook Inlet and a thousand miles west of Juneau. In fact, it is only 160 miles east of Honolulu. The Russians maintained a penal colony there, the convicts operating a coal mine. Indians had come to get supplies of coal, also to catch and dry salmon. On a little island by itself is Mt. Augustine, an active volcano. The sun set like a ball of fire at 9:30. Late in June, the day is twenty hours long and in mid-winter but four hours. A fine aurora borealis was another great sight.

The Return Trip Begins

The Columbia Glacier was visited on the return, also Ellamar, where there is a valuable copper mine, and where the salmon run was so great the visitors caught ten-pound fish with their hands. A few of our party here had opportunity, while the steamer was at the dock, to reach by launch the home of some Natives from the westward, who had built a little village of two or three hundred souls. Here was a Greek church with a priest only lately arrived from Russia. The interior of a Greek church differs from other churches in many ways, the altar being in view only during services, at the other times being covered with a curtain. It is in a sacristy or room containing the robes of the priest and all other paraphernalia for celebrating mass. No woman is allowed to enter this room.

A Good Time at Valdez

Valdez was again visited and a longer stop made. Its people were wild in efforts to entertain, and of course as at other places, there was a dance. It has all that Cordova and Seward have except a railroad, and the United States government is partially compensating for this by building a wagon road to Fairbanks. This is said to be the most northerly, open-winter point in the world and in winter, Yukon and Nome mail goes from here by stage, and further on by dog team. Fort Liscom is located here as well as a United States court-cable-terminal wireless-station, and one or two commissions. It is the point where "sail meets trail." Valdez also has its glacier, a famous one, and an automobile for public use which cost $4,000. Here the steamer took aboard 58 Japanese seal poachers who, having served their sentences, were being deported. One of them died while in jail and his comrades burned the body on a pile of wood, sending one-third of the fragments to his widow, a third to his parents, and burying the other portion.

Short Stop at Metlakatla

A little rough weather was experienced in Prince William Sound the next day and many were sea-sick again. The rest of the homeward trip was as smooth as could be; the weather being perfect. Ordinarily there is rain and fog, but fate was kind and held them back. Although it was a little out of the course, Annette Island was visited. Here an independent lay-missionary, Father Duncan, who has been among them for more than fifty years, has organized several hundred Indians into a cooperative society and they have built the town of Metlakatla, which has a fine church, a good harbor, dock, salmon cannery, saw mill, and industrial shops, all owned and conducted by the natives. The houses are built according to the white man's plan, and are very neat inside. This is a unique community. The presence of white men is not sought, and few come, except to see and go. Cordova and Juneau were also re-visited on the way down, and Seattle reached in time to take the train for home Friday, Aug. 13.

A Country of Great Resources

We are convinced that Alaska has great resources. Besides the gold, the great fisheries and the furs, some of the world's greatest coal fields await transportation facilities for development. There is copper in unlimited amount and the ore is so rich that some of it is hard to work. Lumber, especially spruce, is everywhere in abundance on the coast. Some grains and many vegetables can be produced, enough certainly to maintain a population much greater than the present. The salmon berry and other berries grow in profusion, as do native flowers.

At both Valdez and Seward, fine vegetable gardens were seen and a few little farms. It is said that as far north as the Fairbanks region, there is a place of hot springs where a wide range of products are raised. The heavy winter snows melt there, and moose and caribou come down for food, affording an easy supply of meat for the white man.

The Guggenheims are buying much of the mining property and J.P. Morgan & Co. have large investments. This is centralizing the ownership and putting development on a solid basis. Their engineers have reported vast wealth waiting to be dug out of the ground and they will reap the lion's share of the profit. But many others will make fortunes in Alaska for many years to come and many people will go there to live and be contented.

Meanwhile none have seen this country, who have not made at least a superficial coastal trip of this great territory, which is about a third as large in area of the states in the Union. When the government builds the light houses, which it should, more vessels will be run there. The present travel is increasing their number and no one returns disappointed or unastonished.

Leaving Alaska

Before leaving the steamer "Northwestern" at Seattle, the following appropriate lines, written by Mr. W.H. Greenhow, a member of our party, were read at an "experience" or "thanksgiving" meeting held by the N.E.A.:

"We've sailed thy placid, inland seas,
  We people from the South,
We've breathed thy balm-scented breeze
  As we passed the Dixon's mouth;
The mountains of thy channels crowned
  With everlasting snow
Like escorts ranged along our path
  To point the way to go.

Hurrah, hurrah, Alaska was our goal,
   Hurrah, hurrah, the people with a soul.
We'll sound thy warmest praises,
From Panama to the pole
   As we sail away from Alaska.

From Ketchikan to Treadwell's mills,
   From Treadwell to Juneau,
From Juneau to Cordova's hills
   They kept us on the go.
Where Valdez camps upon her trail,
   Where Seward's pine trees grow
We've met thy people, Alaska.

   Hurrah, hurrah, the land of many showers,
   Hurrah, hurrah, the land of sweetest flowers,
Thy memory will stay with us
As we journey to our homes,
   Regretfully leaving Alaska.

We've seen thy mighty rivers flow
   As we hunted for thy gold,
We've climbed thy copper mountains,
   And we've faced thy glaciers cold.
We've seen thy salmon humping
   Their way up rocky streams,
And the totem poles will haunt us
   As we lie down to our dreams.

   Hurrah, hurrah, we'll sound thy praises meet,
   Hurrah, hurrah, we leave with memories sweet.
We're going to our homes once more,
We're on our sad retreat,
   To dream of thee, Alaska."

Next week we will print a brief but intensely interesting descriptive sketch of Alaska, which we hope each of our readers may take the time to peruse carefully. It will give some idea of the limitless resources of the most wonderful country in the whole world. Thanking you for your patience in reading these rambling observations, gotten together as best I could, I remain,
   Very truly, J.L. Gillespie

Interesting Data
Concerning Alaska
Some History about Wonderful Country and its Resources

Having gotten together and published last week some observations as to our recent twenty-day voyage along the coast of Alaska, we reproduce below an interesting bit of history about Alaska and the trip prepared and distributed among the members of the National Editorial Association by the Alaska Steamship Company. These facts and figures are well worth reading:

"It was on July, 5th, 1741, one-hundred and sixty-eight years and eight days prior to the date for the sailing of the National Editorial Association Excursion for Alaska, that Vitus Bering, after groping his way across the uncharted waters of the Bering Sea and the North Pacific Ocean, sighted the coast of Alaska. Just forty-four days before the discovery of Alaska, George Washington cut down the cherry tree in his father's garden. We know that some unsentimental historians dispute this episode, so familiar to childhood memory, but our researches for the contemporaneous event that would put the date of the discovery of Alaska in display-type, have brought to light the unexpected and astonishing fact that George Washington, then in his tenth year, felled the cherry tree with his little hatchet on July 4th, 1741, to celebrate the third birthday of George III. It is not the province of this folder to discuss whether this little cutting affray had anything to do with the subsequent relations of these historic personages.

"Had this great prize of discovery fallen to any other nation than the one possessing the whole of northern Asia as a frontier, it would not have passed after little more than a century of uncomprehending possession for a sum less than the present value of one season's catch of food fishes along its coast into the reluctant ownership of another nation. As well, might Americans 100 years ago attempted to estimate the value of the Louisiana Purchase as to presume today to forecast the future importance of that great real estate transaction, whereby, at a price a little under two-cents the acre, the United States added to its possessions 375,000,000 acres of unexplored land in the northern part of the continent.

"For thirty years, the traditions of the Russian fur corporation and the prejudice engendered by the political controversy attending the acquirement of Alaska served to keep the people of the United States from coming into the enjoyment of their own. The country was supposed to be valuable only for the rich furs which its land and water animals produced.

"For a quarter of a century, a handful of Alaska pioneers have been telling in a feeble voice that the country is valuable and that it has many great resources; that it is an "empire without a people." The voice of the pioneer is beginning to be heard. We are going to take you, gentlemen of the National Editorial Association, on a brief trip into this new land of promise; and we believe that the journey will delight and astonish you, and we hope when you return to your homes and your work, that you will carry with you facts about the country and memories of a pleasant voyage that will make interesting material for your readers. Maybe you'll add your clarion voices to the feeble voice of the pioneer, and help to correct the misapprehensions concerning Alaska.

"We must travel six hundred miles before we reach Alaska, and in order that you may see the country from a proper viewpoint, we shall ask you to indulge us while we briefly tell you something about this wonderful north land of ours. Alaska has an area of 586,400 square miles. This is greater than the combined area of Washington, Oregon, California, Arizona, and Nevada. It was purchased from Russia in 1867 and cost the United States $7,200,000. Since 1878 the total value of Alaska products is $320,000,000. The value of minerals exported from Alaska during this period is $148,000,000. Gold is the principal item of these minerals. The gold produced would weigh about 284 tons and is valued at $142,000,000. Most of this gold has come from placer deposits.

"There are two creeks in Alaska – Anvil Creek, in the Nome country, and Cleary Creek, in the Fairbanks district – each of which has produced more gold than we paid for the country. The Treadwell mines on Gastineau Channel, with a surface area of not more than 200 acres, have produced gold valued at five times the purchased price of Alaska. There are hundreds of millions of dollars of this valuable metal in sight, and vast regions of unexplored territory. The mineralized-area of Alaska is greater than the entire state of California, and the indications justify the statement that "Alaska contains more gold than California, Australia, or South Africa."

"The comparatively small value of the other mineral products is due to lack of development. The copper mines, excepting a few on the coast, are waiting for means of transportation. Corporations are now expending millions of dollars to provide these facilities. There is more copper in Alaska than has been mined in the United States. Alaska has the greatest copper mine in the world, a mine in which a 200-foot tunnel and a few cross-cats revealed ore that in 1900 had an estimated value of $22,000,000. The ledge of this mine is 110 feet wide and the average value of the copper in the entire ledge is 22 percent. Twenty-five feet of this ledge contains ore which gives an assay value of sixty-eight percent, copper. There are copper nuggets in this region varying in size from a shot to a weight of three tons. We are going to take you in the outskirts of this rich copper region. And there are still other regions of Alaska which contain valuable deposits of copper.

"Alaska contains more coal than Pennsylvania. It contains anthracite coal equal to the best grade mined in the United States. Our journey takes us up in the coal region of Alaska. The combined area of the Bering River and Matanuska coal fields is about 100 square miles. The estimated tonnage from these fields, from present prospects and development, is 1,000,000,000. The United States Geological survey reports 12,644 square miles of coal-bearing rocks in Alaska and an area of 1,238 square miles of coal. No doubt there are many undiscovered coal deposits. The total area of anthracite and bituminous coal is 557 three-square miles and the total area of anthracite and bituminous coal-bearing rocks is 5,990 square-miles. The remainder of the coal is lignite. These data, gentlemen, will enable you to make an estimate of the quantity and possible value of the known coal deposits of Alaska.

"On our journey we shall pass the Kayak, or Katalla oil fields, the most promising in Alaska. And while they have not produced oil in any great commercial quantity, the oil secured is of the best quality; and it is the opinion of experts who have examined these fields, that there is an immense reservoir of oil in the Katalla field. In the early part of our journey we will pass by an island where marble, equal to any in the United States, is quarried, and by another island where gypsum is mined. We will not go to the tin country, as that is in the extreme north-western part of the territory, a region of Alaska that contains the most promising tin mines ever discovered in the United States. Most of the silver that has come from Alaska is a by-product of gold and copper, but there is a large number of galena ledges, carrying a high percentage of silver. These ledges are now in process of development. There are other minerals in Alaska – tungsten, asbestos, mica, cinnabar, graphite, and bismuth – but they have not as yet been produced in commercial quantities. Garnets and rubies have been found in the territory, and on the Kobuk River on the Arctic slope, there is a mountain of jade.

"There are more fish in Alaskan waters than in all the fisheries of the Atlantic Coast. The value of food fishes exported from Alaska since 1878 is $115,000,000. The total value of salmon exported from Alaska is $105,000,000. The value of Alaska's fish product last year was more than $11,000,000. If the cans of salmon put up in Alaska laid end to end, they would reach five times around the earth. The salmon fisheries of Alaska furnish one-half of the salmon product of the world. There are 30,000 square miles of cod in the North Pacific Ocean and in Bering Sea that have been scarcely touched. The halibut fisheries from Dixon Entrance to the Alaska Peninsula are both extensive and productive. The total value of fish by-products from Alaska during the past thirty-years is probably more than $10,000,000. These by-products comprise whalebone, oil, fertilizer, etc. The whaling industry in Alaskan waters since the first Right whale was caught on the Kodiak grounds in 1835, has produced a revenue of more than $100,000,000. The fur product of Alaska, valued at more than

$100,000,000 during Russian occupation, has a value of near $50,000,000 since we acquired the country.

"There are some farms in Alaska – enough to prove that the soil is productive, and fertile, and capable of supporting a population of many millions. There are more than 30,000 acres of homesteaded land in the vicinity of Fairbanks. The great Tanana Valley is adapted to agriculture. The same may be said of the Copper River Valley and the Valley of the Susitna.

"In brief, all of Alaska, south of the Yukon, is destined to become an agricultural country. Why shouldn't it? The latitude is similar to the productive regions of the Scandinavian Peninsula and the climate in some parts of this country is much milder than the climate of northern Europe; the rainfall is adequate, and the soil is fertile. You never ate such vegetables as are grown in the Yukon basin. They have flavor that is distinctive, incomparable.

"The quantity of wild berries that grow in Alaska is one of the pleasing and surprising features of the country. There are hundreds of thousands of acres of fruit-laden bushes which every year shed their delicious burden upon the palateless soil. The principal varieties of berries are blueberries, cranberries, salmon berries, and currants. Bears feast in berry patches and grow fat. Since we acquired Alaska its wasted fruitage would make wine enough to drown the sorrows of the world. If you do not believe us, ask the settler who makes jams and jellies for winter use; ask the Indians of the Yukon and its tributaries who gather the fruit in capacious-birch baskets and enjoy a perpetual feast during the berry season; ask the Eskimos who go berrying on the tundra and treeless hills of Northwestern Alaska and preserve the fruit for winter use by soaking it in seal oil and filling great seal skins with the savory (?) mixture.

"Not many persons know that there is a very promising livestock industry in Alaska. This livestock is neither horses, cattle, sheep, goats, nor hogs – it is reindeer. The day is not far-distant when the markets of the United States will be supplied with delicious reindeer steaks from Alaska. There are 20,000 reindeer in Northwestern Alaska, and the increase is at the rate of thirty-three and one-third percent every year. Within eighteen years there will be more than a million reindeer in Alaska. Reindeer moss in Alaska, upon which the deer subsist in the winter, will provide forage for 8,000,000 reindeer. Reindeer do not have to be stabled, and they provide their own food through all seasons.

"Alaska has vast forests. There are extensive areas of timber which may be converted into merchantable lumber. But the day of lumber exports has not arrived. There has been manufactured in Alaska, for local use, lumber to the value of not less than $1,000,000. There are extensive forests of small trees and soft wood suitable for wood pulp."

The publication of the above concludes our articles on Alaska for the present, but we shall, at different times, make some comments on the progress of that wonderful section of country. We would be delighted to see Alaska twenty-five years hence and view the phenomenal growth and development which we are confident she will achieve within that time, if not at an earlier date.

For the sight-seer, the trip to Alaska is the greatest and most wonderful of any on the globe, and we would advise everyone who can possibly do so, to visit this land of supreme splendor and gorgeous grandeur.

Very truly, J.L. Gillespie

Index

A
Active Pass 63
Adams, Mrs. 6
Alaska livestock industry 33
Alaska bears 33
Alaska berries 34, 47, 56, 69, 73
Alaska Central Railway 61, 62, 68
Alaska farming 53, 73
Alaska fisheries 53, 72
Alaska glaciers 34–38, 59
Alaska mining 29–33, 53, 71–72
Alaska moose 62
Alaskan Elks Clubs 65
Alaska reindeer 73
Alaska Steamship Company 20, 53, 63, 70
Alaska timber 73
Alaska twilight 43
Alaska vegetable gardens 69
Alaska whales 60–61, 65
Alaska whaling industry 72
Alaska wild life 62
Alaska-Yukon-Pacific Exposition 13–18
Albatross 61
Anti-Saloon League 55
Aurora Borealis 40

B
Baker, Dr. Fred and Dr. Charlotte 28
Baranoff, Alexander 41
Beach, Rex 37
Bears. *See* Alaska bears
Bering River, Alaska 72
Bering, Vitus 61, 70
Berries. *See* Alaska berries
Bonanza Copper Mine, Alaska 29–30
Bremerton Navy Yard, Washington 19
British Columbia, Canada 22, 63

C
Cape Hinchinbrook, Prince William Sound, Alaska 60
Childs Glacier, Alaska 36–38, 66, 67
Chimay, Princess 5
Chitina, Alaska 29
Clark, Dr. Louise Harvey 28
Clark, Mr. E. P. 28
Cliff House, San Francisco, California 6
Columbia Glacier, Alaska 68
Cook Inlet, Alaska 61, 68
Copper River, Alaska 28, 66, 67
Copper River Company 29

Copper River Railroad 29, 31, 37, 44, 66, 67
Copper River Valley, Alaska 73
Cordova, Alaska 28, 29, 31, 44, 65, 66, 69
Croskey, Captain Alfred 20, 53, 63, 65

D
Dixon Entrance, Alaska and Canada 63, 72
Douglas, Alaska 26, 64
Douglas Island, Alaska 29, 44, 53
Duncan, William 49, 62–63

E
Ellamar, Alaska 68
Exum, E.W. 67

F
Fairbanks, Alaska 45, 68–69, 71, 73
Fairweather Range, Alaska and Canada 61
Farming. *See* Alaska farming
Ferry Building, San Francisco, California 5
Fisheries. *See* Alaska fisheries
Flickinger, Miss Laura 16
Flickinger, Miss Mary 16
Fort Liscom, Alaska 68
Front Street, Ketchikan, Alaska 25

G
Gastineau Channel, Alaska 71
Gattis, John L. 67
Gillespie, J.L. 70, 73
Glaciers. *See* Alaska glaciers
Götterdämmerung 3
Gould, Helen 43
Greek church 68
Greenhow, Mr. W.H. 69
Guggenheims 69
Gulf of Georgia, Canada 63

H
Hawkins, Mr. 68
Heney, Michael J. 29, 33
Herbert, B. B. 53
Holmes, Elias Burton 21
Hotel Seattle, Seattle, Washington 12
"Humpies" 64

I
Icy Strait, Alaska 65
Indian social clans 56
Inside Passage 57, 65

J

Jancsi, Rigó 5
J.P. Morgan & Co. 69
Juneau, Alaska 44, 60, 64, 69
Juneau Elks Club, Alaska 65

K

Katalla, Alaska 72
Ketchikan, Alaska 22, 22–25, 53, 55, 55–58, 56, 57, 63, 63–64, 64, 70
Ketchikan River, Alaska 56
Khayyam, Omar 21, 26
King, Mr. and Mrs. Lyman 27
Knight, Miss 6
Kobuk River, Alaska 33
Kodac-fiends 58
Kodak picture 62
Kyam totem pole 56

L

"The Lady of Kazan" 42
Le Conte, Professor Joseph 59
Long Beach, California 6, 28
Lott, Mrs. D.B. 67

M

Madrona tree 7
Major, Miss Lutie 17
Matanuska, Alaska 68, 72
Metlakatla, Alaska 49, 50, 62–63, 69
Miles Glacier, Alaska 36–37, 66, 67
Mining. See Alaska mining
Mirror Lake, Alaska 62
Moose. See Alaska moose
Morgan, J.P. 67
Mowich Canyon, Washington 9
Mt. Augustine, Alaska 68
Mt. Edgecombe, Alaska 43
Mt. Logan, Canada 61
Mt. McKinley, Alaska 61
Mt. Rainier, Washington 8–9, 18
Mt. Shasta, California 7–8
Mt. St. Elias, Alaska 39, 61
Mt. Tacoma, Washington 9
Muir Glacier, Alaska 65
Muir, John 6
Muir's Peak, California 7

N

National Editorial Association 19, 20, 53, 63, 70, 71
Newspapers
  The Daily Record, Juneau, Alaska 67
  The Beaver Herald, Beaver, O.T. Oklahoma 54
  The Commonwealth, Greenwood, Mississippi 63
  The Daily Alaskan, Skagway, Alaska 19, 51, 67
  The Ellensburg Dawn, Ellensburg, Washington 18
  The Evening Statesman, Walla Walla, Washington 29
  The Kennewick Courier, Kennewick, Washington 14
  The Leavenworth Echo, Leavenworth, Washington 10
  Printer-Journalist, Chicago, Illinois 53
  The San Francisco Call, San Francisco, California 4
  The San Juan Islander, Friday Harbor, Washington 53
  Waterloo Daily Reporter, Waterloo, Iowa 53
Nome, Alaska 41, 68, 71
Norris Glacier, Alaska 35
Northern Lights 39

O

Olympic Mountain Range, Washington 16
Olympics, Washington 18
Orca Inlet, Alaska 31
Oregon 7

P

Parrott, W.F. 53
Pay Streak, Alaska-Yukon-Pacific Exposition 3, 17
Perkins, G.E. 67
Photographers
  Curtis & Miller, Seattle 8, 24, 50
  Detroit Publishing Co. 2, 21
  H.C. White Co. 6, 7
  Hegg, Eric A. 37, 41, 42, 46
  Kelly, E. W. 12
  Keystone View Company 13, 35
  Park, A. J. 14
  Romans Photographic Company 16
  Sheelor, F.W. 26, 47
  Underwood & Underwood 5, 20, 36
  Winter & Pond 22
Pioneer Square, Seattle, Washington 12
Poodle Dog Cafe, Seattle, Washington 3
Porpoises 65
Port Graham, Alaska 45, 48, 53, 61, 62, 67, 68
Portland, Oregon 6, 47
Port Valdez, Alaska 47
Potter, Miss 28
Prince William Bay, Alaska 66

Prince William Sound, Alaska   60, 69
Puget Sound, Washington   22
Pullman car   1, 3

Q
Queen Charlotte Sound, British Columbia, Canada   55

R
Reindeer. *See* Alaska reindeer
Russia   43, 68

S
Sabbath religious services   43
Salmonberry   47, 56
Salmon fishing   64
Salmon River, Ketchikan, Alaska   22
San Francisco, California   3
San Francisco City Hall, San Francisco, California   4
Sea gulls   61
Seal Rocks, San Francisco, California   6
Seattle dock, Washington   20
Seattle Press Club   53
Seattle, Washington   3, 12, 14, 16, 19
Seward, Alaska   29, 45, 45–46, 53, 61, 61–62, 62, 67, 67–70, 69
Seward's Folly   29
Seward, William H.   29
Shefler, W.H.   67
Shelikov Company   41
Shirley Poppies   17
Sitka, Alaska   41–43
Skagway, Alaska   19, 51, 64–65
Southeastern Alaska   41
Southwestern Alaska   53
"Sparks" (wireless operator)   54
Steamer Alameda   32
Steamer Empress   21
Steamer Minnesota   20
Steamer Northwestern   43, 53, 54, 63, 65–66
Steel, W. A.   20
Stevens Passage, Alaska   35
Strait of Juan de Fuca, Alaska and Canada   63
Strong, Orno   47
Susitna Valley, Alaska   73

T
Tacoma, Washington   19
Taft, President William Howard   14–15
Taku Glacier, Alaska   35–36, 58
Taku Inlet, Alaska   35, 58, 65
Tanana Valley, Alaska   73
Tate-Zincan, San Francisco, California   4
Techau, San Francisco, California   4
Telegraph   54, 60
Thlingit Indians   56
Thousand Islands of the St. Lawrence River   22, 58
Three Sisters Mountains, Sitka, Alaska   41
Timber. *See* Alaska timber
Totem Pole, Ketchikan, Alaska   24
Totem poles   57, 64
Totems   56
Tower, Grace Hortense   21, 26
Travels in Alaska by John Muir   6
Treadwell Mine, Alaska   29, 53, 59–60, 64, 70–71
Tsimshian   49
Tsimshian language   56
Twilight. *See* Alaska twilight

V
Valdez, Alaska   26, 44, 46–48, 60–61, 68–70
Vancouver Island, British Columbia, Canada   63
Vegetable gardens. *See* Alaska vegetable gardens

W
Ward, Clara   5
Ward, E. B.   5
Watson, Mr. Frank   68
W.C.T.U.   55
Whales. *See* Alaska whales
Whaling industry. *See* Alaska whaling industry
White, Mrs. Emma   16
White Pass and Yukon Railroad   29
Wildlife. *See* Alaska wildlife
Windsor Glacier, Taku Inlet, Alaska   36
Wireless   43, 68
Wireless Daily Tribune   54
Wirt, Mr.   28

Y
Yukon, Canada   3, 11, 14, 17, 29, 40, 45, 64, 68, 73
Y.W.C.A.   55

Z
Zech, Miss   6

www.ingramcontent.com/pod-product-compliance
Lightning Source LLC
LaVergne TN
LVHW061217060426
835507LV00016B/1981